KOSOVO CROSSING

AMERICAN IDEALS MEET REALITY ON THE BALKAN BATTLEFIELDS

—————

DAVID FROMKIN

THE FREE PRESS

THE FREE PRESS
A Division of Simon & Schuster, Inc.
1230 Avenue of the Americas
New York, NY 10020

Designed by Ellen R. Sasahara

Manufactured in the United States of America

10 9 8 7 6 5 4 3 2 1

Library of Congress Cataloging-in-Publication Data is available

ISBN 0-684-86889-X

FOR FAREED ZAKARIA
who gets it right every time

CONTENTS

ACKNOWLEDGMENTS

MANY THANKS ARE OWED to a number of people, without whose help, support, and encouragement this book would not exist. In the first instance, the idea of writing this book was proposed to me by Paul Golob, my editor at The Free Press, who oversaw its development through every phase. In the largest sense, this is his book.

Many thanks to Fareed Zakaria for having pushed me to do this project; to Roger Kimball for invaluable logistical support; and to Sara Lussier for cheerfully giving up all her free time in order to type and edit my only barely legible manuscript. I am extremely grateful to the three of them: without them it wouldn't have gotten done.

Many thanks, too, for superefficiency to Alys Yablon, Paul Golob's assistant. Thanks to Paula Duffy, my welcoming publisher who greeted me with talk of friends and places of whom and of which, by happy coincidence, we share memories. And especial greetings and thanks to Mark Gompertz; for years we have been waiting to do another book together, and now we can do it.

And thanks to my Boston University colleagues, Joachim Maitre and Walter Connor, for helpful suggestions, and for supplying me with useful readings.

For friendship beyond the call of duty, thanks to James Chace for reading the manuscript and for being so helpfully critical.

As always, my agent Suzanne Gluck and her assistant Karen Gerwin-Stoopack were indispensable.

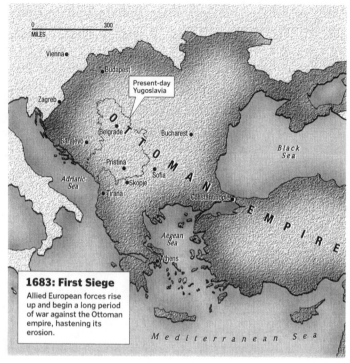

1683: First Siege

Allied European forces rise up and begin a long period of war against the Ottoman empire, hastening its erosion.

Before WWI

The Balkan Wars (1912-13) finish the dismantling of Ottoman rule in Europe, with much of the land going to Servia (Serbia), Greece, Montenegro and Bulgaria. Bosnia later becomes a province of Yugoslavia (1918).

Between The Wars

The creation of Yugoslavia encompasses Serbia and Montenegro as well as former territories of Croatia, Slovenia, Bosni-Herzegovina and Dalmatia.

Today

As an autonomous region (1946), Kosovo became home to more Albanians than Serbs in the late 60's. Resulting tensions have led to the current situation, with Kosovo's partition or the redrawing of Serbian borders looming as problematic options.

KOSOVO CROSSING

PROLOGUE

"THIS IS THE END of the last American war in Europe—and we won it!" an expert on American foreign policy exclaimed happily. His colleague retorted: "It isn't even the end of *this* war, let alone any other; the commitment we've given to Yugoslavia is an open-ended one that we're going to regret."

Though neither wished to be named, they hold their views strongly; and both were reacting to the same news. The news, which broke on June 3, 1999, was that Yugoslavia's president, Slobodan Milosevic, and the Serbian parliament had accepted an international peace plan to bring an end to their conflict with the North Atlantic Treaty Organization (NATO), which had begun seventy-two days earlier, on March 24. In effect the Balkan leaders had capitulated to NATO. They agreed to halt and then reverse their efforts to drive out the ethnic Albanian inhabitants of Serbia's southern province, Kosovo. Six days later, on June 9, a modified version of the peace plan was im-

1

plemented through an agreement between Lieutenant General Sir Michael Jackson, NATO's representative, and representatives of the Yugoslav Army, setting forth the details of Serbia's military withdrawal from Kosovo.

The first article of the peace plan demanded the "immediate and verifiable end of the violence and repression in Kosovo." The plan then called for a quick withdrawal of Serbian forces from Kosovo, which nominally was to remain a province of Serbia, and for a return of the million or so Kosovar refugees to their homes. Eventually, Kosovo was to enjoy autonomy; but in the meanwhile, it would be administered by the United Nations, with an international force of fifty thousand troops to guard the province and its newly returned inhabitants. The troops would operate under a mandate from the United Nations, with Russian participation, and a NATO "core" that would include seven thousand American soldiers, comprising 14 percent of the expeditionary force.

NATO leaders remained wary of Yugoslav intentions, and showed it by keeping up their aerial warfare until the withdrawal of Serbian forces began in earnest on June 10, after a week of fits and starts by Serbia's representatives at the negotiating table. Not even victory looked as though it were going to be easy.

The peace agreement had been a long time in coming. Toward the end, it seemed possible that NATO unity might crack before Yugoslav morale did. A breakthrough, however, seems to have been scored by the U.S. deputy secretary of state, Strobe Talbott, whose patient efforts brought Russia and its representative Viktor S. Chernomyrdin to play a constructive role. In turn the United States and Russia jointly co-opted Finnish president Martti Ahtisaari, whose experience as a Balkan mediator apparently proved invaluable.

When the Milosevic regime announced its surrender, NATO forces had flown more than 33,000 sorties over Serbia using about 1,000 allied airplanes and about 14,000 bombs and missiles. It was the first campaign ever to have been won by airpower alone, despite the warnings of many experts that such an outcome never could be expected. Only three NATO soldiers were killed, all of them in accidents, as against at least five thousand Serbian military dead.

Summarized by such statistics, the war sounds to have been one-sided. But at least three cautionary observations should be kept in mind. The first is that the Kosovo war is one of those episodes in which achieving peace goals, especially over the long run, is likely to prove more elusive and complex than was the achievement of war goals. The second is that disunity within the United States—for this was a highly controversial war—kept the outcome in doubt. The third is that the earlier acts of the drama—the Milosevic regime's first attempts at military aggrandizement in the former Yugoslav states of Slovenia, Croatia, and Bosnia between 1991 and 1995—played out in such a different way as to mislead experts attempting to forecast what might happen in 1999. In particular, the Bosnian experience had suggested that American policy makers were overestimating what military aircraft can accomplish. The

1999 experience suggests that, on the contrary, Americans have been underestimating what airpower can do.

★ ★ ★

At 6:31 in the morning on Tuesday, March 1, 1994, an AWACS reconnaissance plane patrolling the air space over Bosnia spotted six single-seater Jastreb warplanes in a no-fly zone. The Jastrebs belonged to the Bosnian Serb military, which had been fighting against the forces of the Bosnian government for the previous two years. In an effort to limit the scope of the war, the United Nations Security Council had forbidden the Serbs to fly over certain disputed regions in the war-torn former Yugoslav republic. The AWACS had been dispatched by NATO to enforce the UN order. The Jastrebs they sighted on this Tuesday morning were in the act of bombing Muslim positions.

Summoned by the AWACS, two U.S. Air Force F-16 Fighting Falcons of NATO's Southern Europe command, equipped with air-to-air missiles, arrived on the scene and requested and received permission to fire on the bombers. They disposed of the Bosnian Serb warplanes in a matter of minutes. At 6:45, the lead F-16 downed one Jastreb with an Amraam missile, and two minutes later, a second Jastreb with a Sidewinder missile; a minute after that, a second Sidewinder brought down a third Jastreb. Two more NATO F-16s then arrived. The lead F-16 in the new team destroyed a fourth Bosnian Serb warplane while the remaining Jastrebs fled.

It all seemed so easy.

In a telephone news conference afterwards with some of the American F-16 pilots, one of them said, "It wasn't much of a contest." In his view, the obsolete Jastreb warplanes did not stand a chance against NATO's sophisticated weaponry. "That's what your tax money goes for, sir," he told a reporter.

⋆ ⋆ ⋆

In the news dispatches that they filed later that day, journalists reminded their readers that the March 1 air strike was NATO's first. The alliance had been in existence for nearly half a century, yet the sortie over Bosnia was the first occasion on which it had sent its forces into combat.

That was the measure of NATO's success. The North Atlantic Treaty of 1949 had established NATO to *prevent* the outbreak of war, to deter potential adversaries—specifically the Soviet Union—from starting a war in Europe. In all those decades, NATO forces never had been obliged to open fire on the legions of the Soviet empire—which showed either that the threat from the East had not been real, which was difficult to believe, or, as the world, with reason, did believe, that NATO's was a colossal success story. The Kremlin's expansionist ambitions in Europe not merely had been thwarted—which would have been success enough—but had been thwarted without firing a shot.

In retrospect, it seems clear that what happened on March 1, 1994, should have been a warning signal to the

United States and to its European allies. Giving orders, for the first time, to open fire was an implicit confession that circumstances had changed. In the former Yugoslavia, NATO had not done what it was meant to do and what it had succeeded in doing for forty-five years until then. Maybe it wasn't NATO's fault, but it had failed to deter.

NATO airpower was called in again in the Bosnian conflict, and, alongside a successful ground offensive launched by Croatia in August 1995, played a part—though perhaps no more than a supporting role—in forcing the parties to the conflict to sit down at the negotiating table. As such it can be credited with helping to bring about the 1995 Dayton Accords, which resulted in a cease-fire in the conflict.

But in spite of its apparent success, NATO airpower (which is to say, chiefly American airpower) did not perform well enough to restore its credibility as a tool of U.S. policy. When, in 1999, the time came for Washington to threaten Serbia to desist from committing brutalities against the ethnic Albanian population in its southern province of Kosovo, the Serbs dismissed such warnings of incipient air strikes. One sortie by the Americans with their world-of-the-future weapons would not be enough to stop Serbia, nor would many sorties do the job, was the attitude of Serbia's leader, Slobodan Milosevic. And indeed, the bombing of Serbia that began on March 24, 1999, did not cause the Serbs to budge in a day, or in a week, or in a month. They held out for ten weeks.

The great advantage of being able to deter is that a nation can obtain what it hopes to win in a contest of arms without actually having to go through with the contest. In the former Yugoslavia, NATO found that it had lost its credibility. No longer could it deter the other side. Put another way, the Serbs refused to fold in March 1999, so NATO was obliged to play out the hand. Now that it has done so, perhaps its credibility will be restored.

It frequently has been said, and perhaps with reason, that the future of NATO, and of American global leadership, were at stake on the battlefield of Kosovo. Whether or not that puts the case too strongly, the conflict in the former Yugoslavia does afford an invaluable perspective from which to reconsider the questions that have arisen so often in the years following the end of the Cold War, and that are likely to recur in the twenty-first century: when, why, and how should the United States send its troops overseas in an attempt to resolve conflicts if they do not threaten the nation's physical security?

Where will Americans involve themselves next? Does America enjoy such a surplus of power that, after securing its own safety and interests, it can take it upon itself to rescue other peoples all around the world from injustices? And if the United States is so powerful, why on the road that has led from Iraq in 1991 via Somalia in 1993 to the former Yugoslavia in 1999 has America found it so difficult to have its way?

Like a prism, the experience of Kosovo shows the range of possibilities among which the United States must choose as it and the world enter a new age. The Kosovo war raises the question of the extent to which America, in the world outside its borders, has the power to do good— or even whether it knows with any certainty what "good" is.

PART I

POWER AND GOODNESS

1

A VIEW FROM KOSOVO

IN THE SPRING of 1936, a middle-aged British writer
boarded a train in Vienna and set off on a journey to
the Balkans. She was a novelist and journalist who
called herself Rebecca West. The British Council had in-
vited her to lecture in the Kingdom of the Serbs, Croats,
and Slovenes—or, as it had been renamed in 1929, Yugoslavia: the land of the South Slavs. It was to be her first
trip to that country. She did not know the language and
was there to learn.

It was to be a brief visit—only a few weeks long—and
her itinerary was exhausting, with stops at more than a half
dozen cities. Balkan train travel was punishing: the stench
and noise of the cars took their toll, and she was shaken by
the bumpy roadbed.

In touring Yugoslavia, she was accompanied and guided
by the chief of the government's press bureau, who provided information and explanation for what she was seeing. His name was Stanislav, and his father had been a

Polish Jew; but in the book that West later wrote, she renamed him Constantine. It made a better story that way, because she used him as the embodiment of Eastern Christianity.

West returned to Yugoslavia for another brief visit in the following year, 1937, this time with her husband; and then again, by herself, in 1938.

The three trips supplied her with the material that she needed to write *Black Lamb and Grey Falcon,* the highly personal work—part autobiography, part dialogue with her husband, part history, part travel book, part reflections on the basic themes of love, life, war, and politics—that would make her the most famous and most quoted chronicler of this troubled land.

She presented the rugged Yugoslav kingdom as a land of ancient blood feuds and its peoples as haunted by history. To her it seemed appropriate that the Great War should have started there in 1914, and as she was working she sensed that within years—in 1939 or 1940 or 1941—the armies of the greater and lesser powers again would be unleashed in its mountains and valleys, which had been the scene of so much bloodshed in the past.

She used Yugoslavia as a vantage point from which to view the elements that compose mankind's tragic politics. Much of what she thought she saw, and of what she wrote, was from a highly personal point of view that subsequent observers have not always shared. But whatever the merit of her answers, she asked many of the questions that remain relevant today. When we want to have an elucidation of any number of issues regarding Yugoslavia and its impact on great power politics, it is remarkable how often we find that West has been there before us.

★ ★ ★

Indeed, as we enter the twenty-first century, we seem to cross the path of Rebecca West all the time. An example: one of the issues that she explored was the trial by international tribunals of government leaders who formerly had enjoyed legal immunity. *The Economist* reported on April 24, 1999, that in Washington, D.C., an office on the sixth floor of the Department of State now houses an Ambassador for War Crimes: a full-time American official, whose job and title were created only two years ago, and whose function is to monitor official illegalities in conflicts around the world (of which Kosovo is only one) with a view to dealing with them in a court of law, possibly an international one.

The nature of treason was another of her issues. So was nationalism, and its consequences. The modern world, after all, was born of an act of nationalism, the 1914 assassination at Sarajevo of the heir to the Austrian throne by a Serb nationalist that triggered World War I. These were matters that concerned her and concern us too.

But it is the disintegration of Yugoslavia, and the fratricide that followed, that has brought Rebecca West back into the headlines as the twentieth century draws to a close. *Black Lamb and Grey Falcon*, based on her three trips to Yugoslavia and published in 1941, remains a principal source and inspiration for much of what the English-speaking world knows, or thinks it knows, about Serbia, Croatia, Montenegro, Macedonia, Slovenia, Bosnia-Herzegovina, and Kosovo. It is still the book to read on the Balkans. Robert D. Kaplan, the author of *Balkan Ghosts,* the best-selling book on the region that appeared in 1993, wrote that "*Black Lamb and Grey Falcon* drew me to Yugoslavia. . . . My guide was a deceased woman whose living thoughts I found more passionate and exacting than any male writer's could ever be. I would rather have lost my passport and money than my heavily thumbed and annotated copy of *Black Lamb and Grey Falcon.*" He is not alone in this. For good or ill, West has shaped a body of opinion about the origins and causes of the fighting in what used to be Yugoslavia. Whoever writes about Kosovo has to contend with her intellectual legacy.

★   ★   ★

Born to genteel poverty in 1897, Cicily Fairfield, as she then was, came from a mix of Scots and Anglo-Irish ancestry. Her dream was to become an actress, but she lacked both talent and beauty. She was self-conscious about her appearance. She was short—under five foot three—with a broad forehead, intense brown eyes set wide apart, and a dark complexion. Teeth protruded from an uneven mouth, suggesting the predator; at seventeen she claimed to have the "face of a young panther."

She was self-made, and also self-named: she took Rebecca West, an Ibsen heroine, for her pen name. She published her first journalism at the age of nineteen, and quickly became known. "Rebecca had a rough tongue," writes a biographer, and she used it to savage the most famous writers of the day. Of a Scandinavian playwright of towering reputation she remarked, "Writers on the subject of August Strindberg have hitherto omitted to mention that he could not write." Her comments were similarly scathing about George Bernard Shaw, Arnold Bennett, H. G. Wells, and other stars of the literary firmament. This brought her renown. It also brought her introductions.

H. G. Wells, whose acquaintance she soon made (despite her criticisms), occupied a unique position in British cultural life at the turn of the twentieth century. He was a best-selling author of popular novels, and a pioneer of science fiction for the masses; but he also was regarded as a serious writer and an advanced thinker. In the absence of rock stars, Wells attracted what today would be called groupies, and he was notorious for his sexual liaisons with the young daughters of his friends. These affairs usually were initiated by the girls themselves, and he often resisted for a long time—sometimes as long as a year—before succumbing to their advances.

When they met, West was nineteen and Wells was a married man of forty-six. For months, they remained no more than friends and intellectual sparring partners. West then asked for a sexual relationship, which Wells refused. West suffered a breakdown. When she recovered, she published a militant magazine piece ("The Sex War") that ended, "Oh, men are miserably poor stuff!"

Wells described her as a "little disaster of a girl who can't even manage the most elementary trick of her sex." But eventually he surrendered. Months later, Wells informed his wife and took West as his mistress.

The relationship lasted for a decade. During that time, Rebecca West became famous as a novelist. Although her affair with Wells was intended to be clandestine, it was widely known, and added to the glamour of West's name. An American tour by West in the mid-1920s confirmed her celebrity on both sides of the Atlantic.

*   *   *

In world politics there are long periods of rest, during which assumptions are not questioned and normalcy looks as though it will last forever. Then, suddenly, startlingly, like a storm out of a clear blue sky, a moment of truth arrives: foundations are shaken; beliefs are put to the test—and sometimes fail it.

Such were the 1930s, the decade of dictatorships on the march, when Rebecca West decided to write about Yugoslavia as a metaphor for the evil that, in her view, was about to strike Europe and the world. In doing so she achieved her maturity. Rising above the fiction and journalism of her youth, she became the woman of letters with whom we are acquainted today, and who was to influence the thinking of so many.

Central to her vision, and to the half-million-word book that was to be her magnum opus, was a ceremony that she witnessed in Macedonia on her final trip in 1938. It was a fertility rite. Onto an ancient rock infused with the blood of the ages, a gypsy, who had come with his eighteen-month-old daughter, handed up a young black lamb to an executioner, who slit its throat. The gypsy used drops of the blood to make a circle on his daughter's forehead. Then he offered up another lamb to have its throat slit. This was an obligatory thanksgiving because the daughter owed her very existence to the powers of sacrifice. A similar offering on behalf of her barren mother twenty-seven months or so before had brought her into being.

To Rebecca West, this rite was nothing more than "a huge and dirty lie. . . . I knew this rock wall. I had lived under the shadow of it all my life. All our western thought is founded on this repulsive pretence that pain is the proper price of any good thing. Here it could be seen how the meaning of the Crucifixion had been hidden from us, though it was written clear. A supremely good man was born on earth, a man who was without cruelty, who could have taught mankind how to live in perpetual happiness; and because we are infatuated with this idea of sacrifice . . . we found nothing better to do with this passport to deliverance than to destroy him."

To sacrifice others was detestable, but it was detestable, too, to sacrifice oneself. This was the thought that led West to Kosovo, and to a meditation on the darkening politics of the 1930s. The road from Macedonia took her to the battlefield at the Field of the Blackbirds, sacred to Serbs, whose warrior ancestors were defeated there by Turkish invaders on June 28, 1389.

The Serbian legend, narrated in a poem that West's guides translated for her, tells that, on the eve of battle, St. Elijah, in the form of a gray falcon, flew from Jerusalem to the Balkans to offer a choice to Prince Lazar, who led the Serbian forces. Elijah told Lazar that he could have an earthly kingdom or a heavenly kingdom, but not both. If he wanted the earthly kingdom, then he and his troops would be victorious in the coming battle; but if he were willing to lose, and to die along with all his troops, then the other kingdom could be his: a heavenly kingdom that would be eternal.

Lazar chose heaven and eternity, a decision that horrified West five and a half centuries later. It was cruel to sacrifice, and immoral to allow yourself to be sacrificed. It was all very well for Prince Lazar to enjoy the delights of Paradise, but he was wicked to allow his army to lose a battle that, as a result, plunged the Balkans into centuries of rule by Turks.

West was driven to think of her pacifist friends in England: people who were fine and decent, had no violence in them, and thought it could be noble to fall in a lost cause. These friends of hers, she decided, *wanted* to lose, *wanted* to die, and since they were willing for the other side to win, were morally as bad as the other side.

She well knew that as she wrote, civilized Europe was disappearing into the darkness of a long night.

★   ★   ★

Those writers and artists to whom West addressed her words and thoughts had been among the people she most admired, good people who loved "honour and freedom and harmony. . . . Such people I have always followed, for I know that they are right, and my reason acknowledges that by their rule and by their rule only can a growing and incorrupt happiness be established on earth." They were people who labored in the cause of world peace, who were opposed to racial and religious prejudice, who upheld the rights of women and minorities, and who had risen above the narrow ties of class or nationality that still bound others. But there have been good people of their sort in many generations, yet goodness still did not prevail in the world. What had the good people failed to do? What had they done wrong? What had they not done right?

Rebecca West was not alone in asking such questions, for in the aftermath of World War I the leaders of the victorious powers had offered a new vision of international politics and had proclaimed a new era that somehow never came into being. Woodrow Wilson, president of the United States, was, more than anyone else, the person who had inspired the belief that a new age was dawning. He foresaw a world in which there were no more wars, in which governments ruled only with the consent of the governed, and in which peace was based upon justice.

Wilson and the other Allied leaders established a League of Nations to preside over international relations. Public opinion was to be brought to bear to force countries to do the right thing; failing that, economic sanctions would be invoked. This was the theory later known as "idealism."

Much good work was indeed done by the League in the 1920s, but it proved unequal to the challenges of the 1930s. In the wake of the Great Depression, Europe fell prey to mass unemployment, industrial strife, and street violence. Parliaments, unable to cope, collapsed; one country after another turned to dictatorship. Against that background, Adolf Hitler's Nazi Party came to power in Germany, promising to undo the defeat suffered in 1918. At the same time, Soviet Russia loomed as the vanguard of global revolution, and many in Europe saw Joseph Stalin as an even greater threat than Hitler.

The idealists had promised peace and justice, but in the moment of truth, confronted by Fascists and Communists, it became clear that you could have one only at the expense of the other. Either give up pacifism and fight against evil, as Rebecca West counseled, or sacrifice civilization on the altar of peace. But then it turned out that the choice was no choice at all; insatiable Nazi Germany would not let its victims have peace on any terms. By the end of the decade it had become clear that appeasement did not work. Every country in Hitler's way would be invaded, whether it fought him or not.

What emerged from the experience of the 1930s was the perception that, in a sense, all international politics are power politics. That was the perception of the new "realist" theory of international relations as expounded by Reinhold Niebuhr, Frederick L. Schuman, E. H. Carr, and later Hans Morgenthau, Martin Wight, George Schwarzenberger, and Raymond Aron.

It was in such company that Rebecca West posed the question that now must be posed for our day as well. She argued that the best people she knew in politics—people such as the gentle and scholarly Gilbert Murray, professor of Greek and chairman of the executive of the League of Nations Union—lacked the lust for power; and in her view, that was the problem. "I began to weep," she wrote, for high-principled, left-leaning friends. "They were always right, but never imposed their rightness."

As she stood meditating at Kosovo, her friends back home continued to depreciate the role of power in politics. British prime minister Neville Chamberlain presided over a country that seemed to lack the will to fight for power, or even to defend such power as it still had; and West's friends deplored the kind of leaders and peoples who believed or acted otherwise. Indeed, the British public welcomed Chamberlain's surrender at Munich as a triumph.

In this, wrote West, the Gilbert Murrays of the world "prove themselves inferior to their opponents, who do not want to separate themselves from the main channels of life, who believe quite simply that aggression and tyranny are the best methods of guaranteeing the future of man and therefore accept the responsibility of applying them."

Individuals, like countries, who want to shape their future have to take power in order to do it. Of the intellectuals who were her friends in Britain, the good and the kind, she commented sadly that "Not one of them, even the greatest, has ever been a Caesar, as well as his kind self." Nor did she think it likely that a Caesar, informed by a lust for power, was likely to be born a kind person as well.

There was an echo here of *Caesar and Cleopatra* (1898) by George Bernard Shaw, whom West had known for a long time. In the play, Cleopatra secretly has ordered the assassination of a politician she believes to be a dangerous enemy. The man is killed. The dead man's supporters riot, demanding vengeance. Angrily, Caesar turns on Cleopatra: "These knockers at your gate are also believers in vengeance and in stabbing. You have slain their leader: it is right that they should slay you. . . . And then in the name of that right shall I not slay them for murdering their Queen, and be slain in my turn by their countrymen. . . ? Can Rome do less then than slay those slayers, too. . . . And so, to the end of history, murder shall breed murder." [Act IV]

If he searched the entire city, Cleopatra claims earlier, Caesar would not find one person to say that under the circumstances she had done wrong. He replies: "If one man in all the world can be found, now or forever, to know that you did wrong, that man will have either to conquer the world as I have, or be crucified by it."

★   ★   ★

Power and goodness: in the tension between them, West found the meaning of her reporting from a troubled land of clan wars and bloodletting. At Kosovo in the 1930s, she was perplexed by the dilemma of politics: if you were ruthless enough to gain the power to change the world, you probably would lack the idealism to change it for the better. But if you were sensitive and gentle and good, you were unlikely to command enough force to translate your programs into reality.

It is a central problem in politics—now as then.

2

POWERLESS AMERICA

I T WAS TO her own country, Great Britain, that Rebecca West lectured in the 1930s. With even greater justice it could have been the United States. And in fact, in the early 1940s, Americans were given a lecture: they were reproved by realist observers of world politics such as Walter Lippmann, the country's leading newspaper columnist. In *U.S. Foreign Policy: Shield of the Republic* (1943) and *U.S. War Aims* (1944), Lippmann argued that, after the generation of the founding fathers, Americans had forgotten how to think about foreign policy and national security. They no longer remembered that if they staked out a position in world politics, they would need to have the power to defend it.

George Kennan, the career Foreign Service officer who served as the first head of the policy planning staff at the State Department, made similar points in his Walgreen lectures at the University of Chicago, printed in book form as *American Diplomacy 1900–1950* (1951). Like Lippmann, Kennan criticized his countrymen for thinking of international relations in terms of morality and legality rather than power: power, that is, relative to the power of other countries, and relative to the commitments the United States had contracted and to the objectives that Washington hoped to achieve.

Lippmann and Kennan explained that America's physical security in the nineteenth and early twentieth centuries had been assured by a large ocean on either side, and by the domination of those oceans by Great Britain. As it was in Britain's national interest to prevent the other great powers, all of which at the time were European, from making further encroachments in the western hemisphere, the United States in effect enjoyed a sort of free ride: the Royal Navy, in England's own interest, provided protection for the Americas as against all the other great powers. That was something that Secretary of State John Quincy Adams had understood instinctively in the 1820s, when he promulgated what became known as the Monroe Doctrine: a statement by President James Monroe warning Europeans against expansionism on their part in the western hemisphere.

Most Americans in the nineteenth century, however, did not see (or chose not to see) the critical role that the British Navy played in preserving America's "principled" isolation from European power politics. As a result, in the waning years of the century they failed to recognize that their country had become vulnerable when such special circumstances began to come to an end. Germany in 1890 set out to overthrow the existing balance of power in the world by supplanting Great Britain as the world's leader. No longer was it certain that Britain and its Royal Navy could shield the United States from potential enemies across the water.

When World War I broke out in Europe in 1914, a few keen-sighted observers of the political scene, such as former President Theodore Roosevelt, saw that America's interests and national security were bound up with the Allied cause. Not even Roosevelt, however, advocated U.S. intervention in the war. He believed that Britain, France, and Russia, on their own, would defeat the Germans.

By 1916 it no longer was possible to be sure of that, and Roosevelt, had it been up to him, would have gone to war. The American people, however, narrowly reelected President Woodrow Wilson that November, as a peace candidate. Wilson's winning slogan, indeed, was HE KEPT US OUT OF WAR.

Germany launched unrestricted submarine warfare against American shipping at the start of 1917. Germany's "U-boats" were enormously effective in cutting the Atlantic highway that ran from the United States to Britain and France, sinking U.S. merchant vessels. American ships are American territory, so this represented an attack on the United States as well as a challenge to American interests.

So, in April 1917, President Wilson asked the Congress to issue a declaration of war, and the Congress obliged. But the president and the Congress did not bring the United States into the war in order to protect its vital interest in preserving the European balance of power. Rather, it was to defend America's honor that the country was going to fight, the president said, and also to bring about a better world.

In a series of public addresses and communications to the Congress, Wilson spelled out what sort of world that would be. It was to be a world run on principles of justice, in which government would only be by consent of the governed, and in which there would be no more war.

The war ended in 1918. The peace conferences began in 1919. The terms of the peace emerged in the early 1920s. By the late 1920s and early 1930s, Americans had seen enough of the outcome of the war to believe that they had been tricked into participating in it. What they saw was that the Allies, Britain and France, helped themselves to vast amounts of territory in Africa and Asia. It looked as though such imperialist gains were what the Europeans really had been fighting for. The Americans demobilized their armies and disarmed. They did not intend to fight again.

In 1917, they had not understood the real reason why it was necessary to go to war, which was to defend the European balance of power, in which the country had a vital interest. Nor did they understand it in the early 1930s, when, overwhelmingly, American opinion held that going to war had been a mistake.

In 1917, they thought they were fighting to bring an end to the European world's bad old ways. Afterwards, they awakened from the dream to find the dominant powers of Europe as bad as ever.

Americans felt that they had been tricked, and were resolved not to be tricked again.

★   ★   ★

By the 1930s, the United States was thoroughly isolationist
and pacifist, and Americans went back to the beliefs that
they had held before the Great War. They continued to believe that their frontiers were secure because of their own
virtues—ignoring the role of the two wide oceans shielding them, and of the Royal Navy. They also took for
granted the blessing of having non-threatening neighbors
to the north and south, Canada and Mexico. They saw no
reason why other countries couldn't be equally secure
without maintaining armed forces. They blamed other
countries for being unable to live in peace.

It was a view that fit well with the republican political
philosophy that they had inherited from many of the
founding fathers: a belief that wars and armies were not
only to be deplored, but were unnecessary for free societies.

A common and long-standing American belief was
that wars were the result of monarchy. Kings waged wars
for private gain. Peoples had no quarrel with one another,
but were obliged to sacrifice their livelihoods and their
lives to enhance the profits and the glory of their mon-
archs. Worse, to further their ambitions, kings maintained
standing armies even during peacetime, a practice that the
founding fathers viewed as a threat to individual liberty—

not to mention a ruinous expense. For Americans held a special view of politics, economics, power, and war.

The American political philosophy was individualist. The function of the government was to provide a framework of security within which persons could pursue their individual goals in the light of their personal beliefs and with the aim of achieving their own happiness. The state existed in order to serve the people rather than vice versa. It followed that the concerns and claims of the state—politics, in other words—were deprecated. To call someone a "politician" was no praise. "Politics as usual" in the conduct of domestic affairs, and "power politics" in international relations, were routinely deplored. By way of contrast, the production and acquisition of wealth was something that individuals did that was good for both themselves and the community. The economy was thus seen as the true source of national power—the cause of which was advanced by peace, but set back by war.

Henry Adams (1838–1918), man of letters and living witness to America's history, wrote of his countrymen: "Believing that in the long run interest, not violence, would rule the world . . . they were tempted to look upon war and preparations for war as the worst of blunders; for they were sure that every dollar capitalized in industry was a means of overthrowing their enemies more effective than a thousand dollars spent on frigates and standing armies. The success of the American system was, from this point of view, a matter of economy. If they could relieve themselves from debts, taxes, armies, and government interference with industry, they must succeed in outstripping Europe."

*   *   *

In the early 1930s, the mood of the United States was so anti-military that the chief of staff of the U.S. Army prudently wore civilian clothes to work. A public opinion poll of nearly 20,000 American Protestant ministers in 1931 showed 62 percent refusing to sanction or support any future war. In another poll, a third of American college students responded that they would not fight in any future war unless the country were invaded, while more than another third said they would not fight even then.

In 1939, the year that World War II began in Europe, sparked by Nazi Germany with an army of 2 to 3 million men, the United States had an army of 174,000. In terms of numbers, that placed it nineteenth in the world, between Portugal and Bulgaria; but as a percentage of its population the U.S. ranking dropped to forty-fifth—forty-fifth out of much fewer than one hundred sovereign nations. The American army was a horse-drawn force, lacking mobile equipment, and it supposedly drilled with broomsticks for lack of rifles. It lacked ammunition for target practice. It had developed an improved machine gun, but had enough money only to produce one: not one *type* of machine gun, but one gun.

Not even the economy, upon which the country relied for its strength, was functional. It remained in the grip of the Great Depression, which in 1937 was even more severe than it had been when Franklin D. Roosevelt took office in 1933. Germany, the other industrial country hit as hard by unemployment, by contrast had rearmed itself into full employment and industrial recovery.

So as Rebecca West was inspired by her visit to the battleground of the blackbirds at Kosovo to reproach those who would have liked to do good in the world, but who lacked the lust for power—and the power itself—that the other side had, no country deserved the admonition more than the United States. Americans championed the causes of liberal democracy and the rule of law, but had not built up the military forces to back up their words.

How did America get from there to here?

PART II

AMERICA BECOMES

KING OF THE HILL

3

AMERICA SURVIVES BOTH
ENEMIES AND ALLIES

WHEN THE GREAT WAR BROKE OUT in Europe in 1914, most of those Americans who took sides sympathized, so far as we know, with Britain and France. As there were no public opinion polls, solid evidence is lacking. There is no question that there was strong pro-German sentiment in the German-American Middle West, and strong anti-English feeling among Irish Americans in Boston and other big cities. On the other hand, there was solid pro-English feeling in the South. In the population as a whole, those who held political views seemed to be repelled by Germany's militarism.

The United States was willing to sell supplies to any and all, but so effective was the Royal Navy's control of the world's oceans that in practice only goods shipped to the Allies could get through. Without having planned or intended it, therefore, America became the arsenal of the Western democracies in their struggle against the kaiser's Germany.

In the spring of 1917, when the United States was brought into the war by German submarine attacks on American shipping, the bloody conflict in Europe was entering its final stages. Many in Washington assumed that the United States, now that it was a belligerent, would focus on financial support and war production for the Allies, while continuing to leave the battlefield fighting to Britain and France. That is nearly what happened.

But as soon as America declared war, French marshal Joseph Joffre, "the Victor of the Marne," who in 1914 had halted the German advance on Paris, brought a military mission to the United States to discuss the New World's new role; and he asked for the dispatch of one American division to Europe to show the flag. President Wilson decided to honor the request, but wanted to send over a force large enough to serve under an independent American commander.

In asking for a declaration of war, Wilson had made clear that the United States would be not an ally but an associated power. America continued to quarrel with the politics of the Allies, especially with their imperialism. Wilson openly doubted whether the Allies had any good reason for fighting Germany, but America had a quarrel of its own with the Germans, for the U-boat campaign had violated American neutral rights and international law. So the United States and the Allies were bound together in parallel but separate warmaking; and Washington accordingly deemed it essential that the American army fight on its own.

Wilson left it to his chosen military commander, General John J. Pershing, to decide how many troops would have to be called to the colors. At first Pershing thought he might want 1 million men; in the end, he found that he needed 4 million.

To raise, train, equip, and send over to Europe that many men was a task requiring years. It looks as though Pershing's American army might have been ready to launch its initial great offensive against Germany on the western front in the summer of 1919 or even 1920. But hostilities ceased in November 1918, with half the Americans still on the wrong side of the Atlantic awaiting transport, while the half that had made the crossing to Europe was, for the most part, barely bloodied. On Armistice Day the United States, despite heroism in a few battles, had not yet really begun to fight.

At war's end the United States, which in 1914 had been the world's biggest borrower, suffering through a severe economic recession, had become rich on its trade with the Allies. It had emerged, at least for the moment, as the richest country in the world. And, though the families of the fallen felt their pain no less keenly because their numbers were small, America itself had escaped with no damage and only light casualties. Its fields and cities were unscathed. The war had raged and ravaged thousands of miles away.

The other victors fared less well.

Great Britain, having occupied the Middle East and taken the German colonies in Africa, looked to be a major winner. Its empire was at a zenith. But, hidden from view, Britain suffered ruinous losses in the war, economically and demographically.

On the surface, France looked to be another winner. In the 1920s, its army was rated the most powerful in the world. But it never truly recovered from its battlefield losses—and above all from its loss of nerve toward the end. In 1917, French troops bleated like sheep when ordered to attack, and army units mutinied. It is an open question whether the French troops on the western front could have held together much longer had it not been for their belief that the Americans soon would come to relieve and replace them.

★   ★   ★

There was an armistice in 1918, and a treaty of surrender that was imposed on Germany at Versailles in 1919; but neither document brought real peace or settled with finality the question of Germany's claim to predominance in Europe.

In 1939, Germany renewed its bid for mastery, and hostilities resumed after an intermission of about twenty years. The following spring, German troops once again poured across the frontier to attack French and British forces in France.

France had never recovered from the wounds it had suffered in 1914–18; Nazi Germany tore the French Army to shreds in a few weeks in June 1940. It was the end of France as the leading power in continental Europe: a position that it had held, on and off, for centuries. Britain now held out alone against Nazi Germany. It fought to survive, but could not reasonably expect ever again to resume its solitary position at the top of the world's powers. British prime minister Winston Churchill's strategy for keeping his country's greatness was to forge a permanent partnership with the United States.

Nazi Germany thereupon committed a fatal blunder: it invaded Soviet Russia on June 22, 1941. One of the most savage—perhaps the most savage—of humanity's large-scale wars ensued. Four years of fighting and slaughter would devastate the Soviet Union seriously and Nazi Germany fatally. Germany thereafter neither wished to remilitarize and contend again for world power, nor felt able to do so.

The United States entered the war in December 1941, after the Japanese attack on Pearl Harbor. The mobilization of men and of the economy took about the same amount of time as under Pershing in 1917–18, but this time the war's outcome was still in doubt when American troops entered the lists in North Africa and the South Pacific. It would take until June 1944 for the Allies to regain a foothold in France and another year before Germany and Japan were defeated—the latter by means of the first use of atomic weapons.

At the end of World War II in 1945, the United States

once again found itself far better off than it had been at the beginning of the conflict. Going to war had lifted it out of the Great Depression and had made it again the richest country in the world. The victorious America of 1945 was even more rich and even more dominant in terms of world trade and production than had been the victorious America of 1919.

Once again the country had entered the war late, after others already had suffered high losses. Once again, the mainland United States had not been touched by the fighting, while the cities of Europe and Asia were being bombed and leveled.

So, as he looked about him as the war drew to a close, President Franklin D. Roosevelt (and his successor, Harry S. Truman) saw only two countries of which the United States needed to take account in creating and maintaining the structure of the postwar world: Great Britain and the Soviet Union.

★   ★   ★

In the mid-1940s, Washington recognized three great powers—and then there were two. Great Britain did not wait to be pushed out, as others had, but instead withdrew in favor of the United States. In an unusual—perhaps even unique—act of enlightened realism, Britain, the supreme world power for generations, handed over its top position to its successor consciously, deliberately, and, in a sense, voluntarily. The ungrudging way in which the move was made reflected the existence of a special bond between the two countries.

The turning over began in the darkest days of World War II. When proclaiming "the American century" in *Life* magazine in February 1941, Henry Luce quoted approvingly a current issue of *The Economist* of London as saying: "If any permanent closer association of Britain and the United States is achieved, an island people of less than 50 million cannot expect to be the senior partner. The center of gravity and the ultimate decision must increasingly lie in America. We cannot resent this historical development."

Once the United States entered into an alliance with Britain in World War II, the partnership between London and Washington did indeed take that shape. On December 22, 1941, only a fortnight after the Japanese attacks on Pearl Harbor, Prime Minister Winston Churchill and his entourage flew to a three-week conference in the New World code-named ARCADIA. In the course of ARCADIA the two countries agreed to establish a Combined Chiefs of Staff to direct their armed forces worldwide; and the British agreed that these supreme commanders should be located not in London but in Washington. It was a partnership, then, weighted toward the Americans, as the alliance's day-to-day military decisions were to be made in the United States.

In September 1943, Churchill proposed to Roosevelt that after victory had been achieved, this wartime arrangement of a joint high command located in the United States should continue, initially on a ten-year renewable basis, but in the hope that one day it might become permanent. "Roosevelt liked the idea at first sight," the prime minister reported to his colleagues and to King George VI.

Though Churchill often was derided as a romantic reactionary, an unabashed imperialist unwilling to recognize the harsh realities of the twentieth century, he showed himself in this respect able and willing to face facts. He saw at the time that Britain had lost its place as the world's foremost power—and had lost it permanently. Relative economic decline was a main cause of this; but it also was a part of the price that fate exacted from England for having fought the two world wars, from start to finish.

Not all British officials agreed with Churchill that global supremacy had been lost. In 1945, it was the view of the Foreign Office that Britain still possessed "all the skill and resources required to recover a dominating place in the economic world." Sir Henry Tizard, chief scientific adviser to the Defence Ministry, was closer to the mark a few years later when he noted, "We persist in regarding ourselves as a Great Power, capable of everything and only temporarily handicapped by economic difficulties. We are not a Great Power and never will be again."

Churchill evidently hoped to maintain his country's global position by leaning on the Americans. But his Labour successors in office (1945–51) chose instead to wind down global positions when they found they could not afford them.

Surprisingly, the exact date and place on which Britain handed over to the United States has been pinpointed both by participants and by historians. It was in Washington in the late afternoon of Friday, February 21, 1947: a cold, gray, and rainy day. It was then that the first secretary of the British Embassy delivered to the Department of State a note that later was to become famous. State was unprepared to receive the message that the note contained; but, appropriately, the department was in process of moving to the new and larger quarters that it would need as America's world role expanded.

The note told the American secretary of state, General George C. Marshall, that Great Britain no longer could shore up the West's position in the eastern Mediterranean in the face of a hostile Soviet Union. British aid to Greece and Turkey, both of which appeared to be threatened by Russian expansionism, would terminate March 31. If the United States wished to take Britain's place, it should prepare to do so effective April 1.

In a burst of energy and creativity, the American government responded that spring by formulating the Truman Doctrine, the Greek-Turkish aid program, and the Marshall Plan. The United States took hold of the torch that had been handed over and ran with it.

But a major driving force was not American but British: Ernest Bevin, foreign secretary in Clement Attlee's Labour government. Like many Western European and American leaders at the time, his principal worry was that the United States would withdraw into isolation after World War II, as it had done after World War I. The evident goal of Bevin's foreign policy was to involve America in securing the defense and revival of England and Europe—and to commit the Americans not in one area alone, but in a broad alliance.

It was Bevin who initiated the European response to the Marshall Plan, first by approaching France, with which England had signed a treaty of alliance the year before, and then, together with France, by inviting the other European countries to meet and enter into a dialogue with the Americans. It was Bevin, too, who organized a European mutual defense league; and after Norway asked for support when threatened by Russia in 1948, he was able to draw the Americans into a security arrangement formalized the following year as NATO.

The United States did not seek leadership; world leadership was thrust upon it, largely by Britain.

* * *

At midcentury there were only two superpowers, the United States and the Soviet Union, and the world was divided between them—except for an amorphous group of the relatively poor and powerless trying to stay free of domination by one or the other rival camp. The two giants were in a growing conflict: a widening encounter that became known as "the Cold War," a name coined by, or at least popularized by, Walter Lippmann. The meaning and conduct of the Cold War changed over the years, but in the beginning its focus was the postwar map of Europe and, above all, the fate of Germany. If the Germans were to be drawn into the orbit of one superpower or the other, that could decisively tip the global balance of power.

The Cold War had its origins in the years immediately following World War II. By 1950 most Americans, government and people alike, were persuaded that the Soviet Union was an expansionist power, aiming to dominate at least the Eurasian landmass and probably the entire world. The Soviets were perceived as posing a military threat not merely to their immediate neighbors but also to the United States. As leaders of a worldwide Communist movement, they fomented subversion in Western and pro-Western countries and posed an ideological threat as well to open societies. America saw its own role as standing guard to repel attacks and advances by the Soviets or their allies around the world.

As Americans saw it, the Soviet Union had been responsible for dividing the world in two. The regimes that the Soviets had established to seal off the frontiers of their sphere constituted, in Winston Churchill's metaphor, an "iron curtain." The curtain cut off Soviet subjects from the free flow of Western words and ideas, which Americans believed would otherwise undermine Soviet authority. The visible symbol of the cutting off was the wall the Russians erected in 1961 to divide their occupation zone in East Berlin from the rest of the city. Two million people had fled the horrors of Soviet rule through Berlin before the wall was built; now it would keep the dissident people in and the subversive ideas out.

Through the succeeding decades it was difficult to

imagine circumstances in which the Berlin Wall could be pulled down. When Ronald Reagan traveled to Berlin in 1987 and admonished the new Soviet leader, Mikhail Gorbachev, to "tear down that wall," his words were widely viewed as Cold War rhetoric. Indeed, as late as January 30, 1989, *Newsweek* magazine cautioned that, despite the liberalizations introduced by Gorbachev, demolition of the Berlin Wall "won't happen soon."

At about that time, the late Raymond Aron, sociologist and political philosopher, addressed the International Institute for Strategic Studies in London on problems of Western security and the Soviet Union. Aron reminded his listeners of the cynical distinction drawn by Machiavelli in the sixth chapter of *The Prince:* "All armed prophets have conquered and unarmed ones failed." But what happens, asked Aron with regard to the Soviet Union, if the armed prophet seizes power by force of arms, remains in power, retains his arms, and continues to use them for repression, but then loses his belief in his prophetic message? What happens if he keeps his military and police machine but loses his faith? That question, as it turned out, was the key to what happened within the Soviet empire.

It crumbled before our eyes. Behind the Iron Curtain in 1989 hundreds of thousands of people took to the streets, crying out for freedom. Neither police nor armies tried to stop them. Swept away by the human waves, the hard-line leaders of Soviet satellite regimes resigned. Travel restrictions were lifted. In November the wall came down, and mobs surged freely into the West.

A commonly repeated jest about the Soviet labor force was that the workers pretended to work and the government pretended to pay them. Now, from the factory floor to the corridors of the Kremlin, it became clear that nobody seemed to believe in what they had been doing. The Soviet system was revealed to be an empty shell.

In 1989, the Soviet Union ended the Cold War by giving up the lands it had occupied during World War II. Two years later, it dissolved itself into its constituent states. And on August 31, 1994, the last Russian troops left German soil, so that the European conflict that began in August 1914 at last was settled.

One of America's leading historians of the Cold War, John Lewis Gaddis, having studied the new materials now available from Russian and other archives, has made a disturbing observation. Gaddis argues that future historians of the Cold War will see the conflict largely as an ideological struggle, their views colored by the way the conflict ended. "The events of 1989–91," he writes, "make sense only in terms of ideas. There was no military defeat or economic crash; but there was a collapse of legitimacy." Those scholars who since the 1940s have urged Americans to think of international conflicts in terms of power and of interests must now, according to Gaddis, revise that view.

A worrisome message, for Americans always have been all too ready to ignore factors of power and interest in international affairs. Unlike dominant powers in the past, the United States did not defeat its rivals; for the most part they fell by the way. Americans, instead of seizing power, have had it handed to them, first by the British, then by the Soviets. History had not taught them lessons in power, for the United States rose to the top by surviving rather than by winning. This has been a dangerous omission in the country's education.

For now, in defining their country's role and mission in world affairs in the coming era, nothing is more important for Americans than to appreciate the extent, the limit, and the uses of their unprecedented national power.

4

MEASURING AMERICA'S
GREATNESS

THE UNITED STATES enters the Christian Era's third millennium as the dominant state in the world.

Its army, its navy, and its air force are all stronger than those of any other country. Military strength in the modern world is rooted in the national economy; here, too, the United States is supreme. Its technology, giving rise to its inventory of space-age weaponry, is far in advance of that of other nations both in quality and in quantity. American soldiers thus have available to them arms and devices that other countries' armies do not have. Moreover, the United States enjoys the ability to project its power—that is, to transport and deploy its forces—in every part of the world. It is not simply a superpower, but the *only* superpower.

When selecting foreign policy goals and framing policies, a country must evaluate its comparative power position with respect to the other countries involved. Whenever the United States has done so in the past decade—when it has measured itself against Iraq, Somalia, Haiti, Serbia, or any other country with which it has come into conflict—it has discovered a vast disproportion: America dwarfs them all in many if not most of the categories that measure international power.

There is *geography*. The United States is favored by ocean frontiers, three thousand miles to the east and six thousand miles to the west. Though oceans offer less protection than they did in the pre–ballistic missile age, they still to a large extent shield the country from enemies in Eurasia. The continental United States occupies a territory of 3.6 million square miles, and its sheer size gives protection of another sort, as size so often did in the past to Russia, China, and India: should a hostile power mount an invasion, there is room in which to retreat and regroup. And in the nuclear age, there still is no bomb in any nation's arsenal explosive enough to destroy more than a segment of the American continent.

In *food and natural resources,* other constituents of national power, the United States enjoys abundance; and in *industrial capacity* it has no superior. It also outnumbers its opponents: its *population,* upward of 250 million, far exceeds those of the countries with which it has dueled since the end of the Cold War, such as Haiti and Somalia. Iraq, for example, is estimated to have only one-tenth the number of inhabitants as America.

America also is ahead of its adversaries in ways that are less easily measured. One of those is the *quality of its gov-*

ernment and politics. As an open society operating under the rule of law, the United States provides an environment that attracts talented people, brings in investment, and promotes science, productivity, and progress. As a liberal democracy, it can also mobilize its population in support of its policies.

The *quality of leadership* is another intangible element of national power in which the United States in the past decade has surpassed the nations with which it has been in armed conflict. Surely not even the most partisan denigrator of George Bush or Bill Clinton imagines them to be intellectually and morally inferior to the leaders they have opposed in Iraq, Panama, Haiti, Somalia, or Yugoslavia.

Other countries display only one or more of the aspects of power. For example, Saudi Arabia is a natural resources power, controlling much of the world's oil reserves. But in military terms, it is no power at all; it would be vulnerable to a takeover from within or without if the United States were to stop protecting it. Japan is an industrial power, but it too operates behind an American shield. North Korea may have a powerful army, but it is weakened by poverty and the ever present threat of starvation.

Only the United States is in all essential respects a great power. But it is the most unusual great power in human history, for the country did not consciously seek such a role in the world. The American political tradition has not revolved around a belief that the nation requires global power to achieve its goals. And when America has failed to obtain what it wants in the world, such an outcome is rarely attributed to a lack of power. In short, the United States has never really learned the facts of international life.

★ ★ ★

In bygone days, children often played a game—do they still?—called "king of the hill." It was played in any one of the many vacant lots that used to dot the cities of the United States. There always was at least one heap of dirt that had been dumped somewhere on the lot, and that a child with a good sense of balance could stand on top of, however precarious the perch. The other children then would gather together and rush him. The object of the game was to knock him off, and then to take his place by pushing all the others off, too.

Rarely did anybody stay on top of the hill long enough to wonder what good it did for him to be there. The United States today is in that curious position.

PART III

WHEN AND WHERE SHOULD

AMERICA INTERVENE

ABROAD?

5

THE FACTS OF

INTERNATIONAL LIFE

I N THE EARLY PART of the twentieth century, American thinking about the country's role in world affairs was dominated by the rivalry of two larger-than-life figures. In large part, that rivalry has continued to dominate the debate ever since.

Theodore Roosevelt (1858–1919), restless and exuberant, was an explosive bundle of energy and talent. A weak and sickly child who had made himself tough, he was a patrician Harvard man who had tamed his own corner of the Wild West. He did it with a rifle in his arms and a Tolstoy novel in his saddlebags. He raised six children, spoke seven foreign languages, and wrote fourteen books. A hero on the battlefield for his exploits as commander of the Rough Riders in the Spanish-American War, he also was awarded the Nobel Peace Prize for negotiating an end to the Russo-Japanese War in 1905.

Roosevelt served as president from 1901 to 1909 and wanted the United States to become one of the great powers, on a par with those of Europe. A nationalist, he briefly flirted with the idea of creating an American empire, particularly in 1902 when he stage-managed a revolution in Panama to gain the Canal Zone for the United States. "I took the canal," he famously said, "and let Congress debate." He took an expansive view of the Monroe Doctrine, and would have been happy for America to dominate the entire western hemisphere, to the exclusion of Europeans.

TR, as he was called, looked at international politics through the worldly and unillusioned eyes of a European, an American version of the German chancellor Otto von Bismarck or the British prime minister Lord Palmerston. But as an American, he also had his visionary side. He wanted to use American power to make a better world. He envisaged an international society that was stable because a cartel of great powers would agree to act in concert to impose their will on the planet, solving problems and keeping order. His notion was to be the genesis of the Security Council concept of the United Nations, later brought into existence by his distant cousin Franklin Delano Roosevelt.

Many of America's most talented young people rallied to TR's banner in his 1912 insurgent bid for the presidency on a third-party ticket, but later abandoned him for Woodrow Wilson (1856–1924), who narrowly won the three-way election with a plurality of the votes. (Finishing third was the incumbent president, William Howard Taft, who had once been TR's protégé.) TR despised Wilson as too weak. Wilson feared TR as too bold.

Whereas Roosevelt was an instinctive internationalist, Wilson was an instinctive isolationist who believed that the

United States was too good to let itself be involved in the sordid politics of the rest of the world. Americans, he felt, would be soiled by taking part in power struggles or wars.

The grandson of a pastor and the son of a Presbyterian minister, Wilson was an academic political scientist who was elected to the presidency after a career in politics of only two years. He was rather like a theologian and not in the least like a politician. Proud, reclusive, and high-minded, he was something of an enigma to his contemporaries and has remained an enigma to historians.

In bringing the United States into World War I in 1917, Wilson was the author of the doctrine that largely has guided the country in foreign affairs ever since. It is the doctrine that if the United States is forced against its will to participate in political or military activities outside the western hemisphere, it should do so with the aim of changing the world: of changing it into a better world.

As soon as America entered the war, Wilson began setting out in public statements the goals and ideals that he proposed to bring to the planet when the United States triumphed—such as open diplomacy, free trade, and the establishment of a postwar peacekeeping organization. Young admirers such as the journalist Walter Lippmann wrongly assumed that the president secretly had devised some strategy for securing the agreement of the Allied countries to pursue, or at least accept, his visionary proposals.

At the Paris Peace Conference in 1919, it transpired that no such thing was true. The president held out high hopes, but had not given thought as to how to achieve them. In fact, he had brought along no contingency plans for dealing with the Allies. He was apparently operating on the assumption that the manifest goodness of his aims would be sufficient to carry the day. He learned at the conference that Britain, France, and the other victorious Allies would pursue their national interests as they interpreted them. Realistic observers could hardly have been surprised that France, having borne the brunt of the fighting on the western front, having suffered the most casualties, and having kept in existence what was considered to be the largest and most powerful land army in the world, would impose its own views as to what was to be done with defeated Germany. Those views did not embody Wilsonian principles.

Wilson and his followers, however, were surprised and disillusioned. Many Wilsonians became ex-Wilsonians.

★   ★   ★

Americans experienced a replay of that disillusionment a quarter of a century later, when World War II came to an end. With the defeat of fascism in Europe and Asia, many expected that, at last, such American goals as having all countries ruled with the consent of the governed would be realized. After all, hadn't the United States won the war?

The answer was that, in large part, it hadn't. The bulk of the fighting—and of the dying—had been done by the peoples of the Soviet Union. Moreover, the Red Army, which was not demobilized after victory as was the U.S. Army, remained the world's largest and strongest—and it occupied the countries of Central and Eastern Europe that it proposed to dominate.

The American Congress and the American people were not prepared for a continuation of hostilities. They had not been told that the Soviet Union aimed at expanding its empire, only that the Russians were our allies against Hitler. They had turned a blind eye to the fact that the Soviet regime was a brutal dictatorship, not much better than that of the Nazi enemy. And they had not realized that at the Yalta Conference in February 1945, Franklin Roosevelt and Winston Churchill had recognized that after the war Eastern Europe to some extent would fall within the Russian sphere of influence.

Above all, they did not match ends against means. They did not understand that there were limits as to the favorable outcomes the United States could obtain outside its borders; and that those limits were the expression of relative power. To take Eastern Europe away from the Red Army in 1945, Americans would have had to go to war against the Soviets—and would have had to win that war.

Americans had failed to learn from Theodore Roosevelt that international relations are about power, not goodness. It was a kind of perverse Wilsonianism that led a significant segment of American opinion to believe that Eastern Europe had been given to the Soviets at Yalta— when in fact it had been taken by them on the battlefield.

Could Americans intervene abroad to change the world? The answer was yes, but only if they had the power to do so, and were prepared to pay the price.

6

THE CONTAINMENT OF THE
UNITED STATES

THE LONG-TERM STRATEGY that the United States employed in its post-1945 rivalry with the Soviet Union was popularly called "containment." It followed from the view that the Soviets would expand wherever they were not opposed. This description of Soviet conduct made its first appearance in a memorandum addressed to President Franklin Roosevelt, dated January 29, 1943, from William C. Bullitt, who had served as America's first ambassador to the Soviet Union in the 1930s. According to Bullitt, the Soviet Union "moves where opposition is weak. He stops where opposition is strong. He puts out pseudopodia like an amoeba. . . . If the pseudopodia meet no obstacle, the Soviet Union flows on."

George Kennan, one of the brilliant young Foreign Service experts who had served in Bullitt's Moscow embassy, and who had helped shape Bullitt's views, wrote along similar lines immediately after the war, when he was re-posted to the Moscow embassy. In February 1946, he responded to a relatively routine request from the Treasury Department for an explanation of Russian behavior by writing a lengthy cabled response warning that the USSR was a hostile and expansionist power. The powerful secretary of the navy, James Forrestal, seized what became known as the Long Telegram and helped make it official American doctrine. It was outlined for the public in a *Foreign Affairs* article, "The Sources of Soviet Conduct" (July 1947), written by Kennan under the pseudonym of "X."

In the "X" article, Kennan described Soviet behavior as the exertion of pressure all around the frontier in "a fluid stream" designed to fill "every nook and cranny" where it was not stopped. To meet this pressure, Kennan advised, America should undertake "a long-term, patient but firm and vigilant containment of Russian expansive tendencies" that would employ "counter-force" against the Soviet use of force. Eventually, he argued, if the United States held the line—and did more than hold the line—the Soviet system might well collapse from within, a victim of its own internal contradictions.

Kennan later claimed that his doctrine was misunderstood; that, among other things, he had intended it to call for political rather than military action. But one way or another, the strategy was employed, and the strategy worked.

★   ★   ★

When the "X" article appeared in *Foreign Affairs*, Walter Lippmann responded to it in a series of newspaper columns that he assembled into a slender volume entitled *The Cold War*. He attacked the containment doctrine from many angles.

One of Lippmann's points was that the United States lacked the forces to patrol the entire circumference of the Soviet frontier. It therefore would have to ally itself with a number of the small states or other minor powers neighboring the USSR to fill in the gaps. The containment policy would thus be dependent on "recruiting, subsidizing, and supporting a heterogeneous array of satellites, clients, dependents, and puppets. The instrument of the policy of containment is therefore a coalition of disorganized, disunited, feeble or disorderly nations, tribes, and factions."

America, Lippmann observed, could not be choosy if it adopted a containment strategy. If a dictatorship were opposed to the Soviet Union, the United States would have to support it. America's clients and allies would have to be "white-washed" and "seen through rose-colored spectacles," for they might well be brutal or corrupt themselves.

In the nineteenth century, long before it became a great power, the United States was free to break off relations with countries that trampled on human rights or offended its principles in some other fashion. Now the United States, even though much more powerful, enjoyed less freedom of action to support its own principles abroad. Containment, in Lippmann's view, condemned Americans to ally with governments that decent people ought to be ashamed of— and then to pretend that these were regimes to be admired and supported. This was precisely what would come to pass in the superpower proxy wars of the 1960s, 1970s, and 1980s.

Of course it could be retorted that America's new allies would be no worse than Russia's. On the other hand, neither would they be any better than Russia's. Was there a point to acquiring more power if it meant you were less free to be good?

★   ★   ★

In yet another way, standing guard against Communist Russia involved restricting America's freedom of action. Like it or not, the United States would have to have what the founding fathers had freed it from: big government, centralized government, large armed forces, high taxes, restrictions on privacy and on the open society.

With his curious ability to get things only half right, Woodrow Wilson in 1919 foretold how the United States would change. He said that if America failed to join an international league, it would have to defend its interests on its own, obliging future presidents to be alert to the threat of war all the time, ready on a moment's notice to order whatever action might be necessary. "You can't do that under free debate," Wilson admonished. "You can't do that under public counsel. Plans must be kept secret."

So a president might have to order American troops into a combat situation before asking the Congress or telling the public. To know when and how to act, the government would need to establish an extensive spying system. Moreover, the United States would have to maintain a standing army and a permanent industrial complex producing military supplies so that its equipment would always be up to date.

Wilson was right about what would happen, but wrong about why. The Central Intelligence Agency, the Department of Defense, the Joint Chiefs of Staff, the staggering peacetime military budgets, the military-industrial complex, and the tendency of our presidents to act first and ask Congress for support only later, all came about, but this was after America joined an international league, the United Nations. They were the product of the internationalist 1940s rather than, as Wilson had supposed, of the isolationist 1920s. Their coming about had nothing to do with whether America joined a league; it had to do with whether it joined the world. The United States could have remained the country it used to be only by genuine isolationism: by withdrawing into the western hemisphere, if indeed that were possible. It was by participating fully in world affairs that the U.S. government changed in the ways that Wilson predicted.

Once again power dictated its own requirements, and thereby diminished freedom. Rebecca West's assumption, that power would bring with it a freedom to accomplish whatever was desirable, was not always true.

★   ★   ★

Americans, government and people alike, were conscious that in world affairs they were engaged in containing the expansionism of the Communist powers: Russia at first, and then China as well. But few in Washington or out recognized that, in turn, the Communist powers were containing the United States.

This flaw, a manifestation of America's persistent refusal to think of foreign policy in terms of power realities, showed itself in the Korean War, the nation's first military intervention abroad following the adoption of Kennan's containment doctrine.

Korea is an Asian peninsula that runs south from northern China into the ocean, like a finger pointed downward. During World War II, it was liberated from Japanese rule by the United States and the USSR. The U.S. Army driving north and the Red Army driving south met halfway at the thirty-eighth parallel, which was intended to be a temporary line of demarcation. Above that line, the Soviets installed a Communist regime headed by Kim Il Sung. Below it, the Americans supported the authoritarian regime of the aging nationalist Syngman Rhee.

On the weekend of Saturday, June 24, 1950, Washington learned that North Korea had launched an attack across the demarcation line. As American government leaders returned to Washington Sunday and Monday for urgent meetings, the news went from bad to worse: in a blitzkrieg, tanks from the North had torn through the defenders and smashed their way south. The South Korean forces were practically on their own, for only an American Advisory Group of five hundred officers and men was stationed in Korea; all other American troops had been evacuated the year before.

The first politically significant advice sent to Democratic president Harry Truman and Secretary of State Dean Acheson came from John Foster Dulles, the de facto foreign policy spokesman of the Republican Party. "U.S. force should be used," Dulles cabled. And it was.

In the two world wars, and even in the Spanish-American War, Americans had been attacked, or believed they had been attacked. The founding fathers had made provision only for the common defense, and it was a widespread belief that the United States would take up arms only in self-defense.

So, in sending troops to Korea, Truman was breaking decisively with the past.

America's leaders drew the inference—correctly, as we now know—that North Korea would not have launched its attack without the approval and, indeed, encouragement of the Soviet Union and China. Although the United States was sending its own soldiers to counter those of a mere proxy, America's armed response could be seen as a military extension of the containment doctrine.

The Korean War was more forcefully presented to the American public as a response to aggression. It had been Woodrow Wilson's plan, in the Covenant of the League of Nations, that if one country invaded another, all the other states would combine—presumably under American leadership—to repel the invading force, restore the frontier, and return to the status quo as it had been prior to the aggression. Wilsonians had woven the same design into the Charter of the United Nations in 1945.

As it happened, the Soviet envoy was absent from the

UN Security Council in 1950 on the day when the United States asked that action be taken in Korea. Therefore, no Soviet veto blocked the Americans. At the time, the Beijing regime did not occupy China's seat in the United Nations, which was held by Chiang Kai-shek's Nationalist government in Taiwan. So there was no Chinese veto either. Free to wage war under the banner of the United Nations, Truman's administration did so, with bipartisan support (for a time) within the United States.

It was as Wilson would have wanted it to be. Truman admired Wilson; and Dulles, as an undergraduate, had been a student of Wilson's at Princeton. But in the giddiness of initial success, neither man remained true to Wilson's austere doctrine.

The turning point came when the United Nations' armies, under the brilliant leadership of General Douglas MacArthur, drove the North Koreans back to the thirty-eighth parallel—and kept on going, instead of stopping there, as the Wilson doctrine required. MacArthur led his forces to the Yalu River, the Korean frontier with China.

Suddenly, hordes of Chinese troops poured across the Yalu; and in disarray, the shattered Americans and their allies fled south.

The disaster should have served as a reminder to the United States that the veto in the UN Security Council is more than a procedure; it is the expression of, and a metaphor for, an underlying power reality. Translated from the language of lawyers into that of laymen, it reads something like this: If we are to keep another world war from breaking out, no great power or powers will take military action in the outside world if another great power or powers will fight to block it.

The human waves of Chinese soldiers that over-whelmed MacArthur's defense perimeter were a sort of veto. What they were saying was that the American army could move north from the thirty-eighth parallel only at the price of starting a war with China.

Quickly understanding the implications of what had happened, MacArthur saw that there was no way of defeating an enemy that always could go back to replenish itself from a seemingly inexhaustible supply of manpower. "Outnumbered" was almost too weak a word to express the size comparison between the UN expeditionary force and China's 1 billion people. To win the war, MacArthur concluded, he would have to reach behind and beyond North Korea: he would have to defeat China, and indeed by his logic he ought to have been prepared to take on, and defeat, the Soviet Union at the same time. To do these things, MacArthur argued, he would have to be allowed to use atomic weapons against China.

His superiors would not allow it. He himself was fired for insubordination.

The United States settled for a draw in Korea, which became available in 1953, in the interregnum following the death of Joseph Stalin. Under the Wilson doctrine, it was all that the United Nations was entitled to achieve. But there was a major flaw in the doctrine: if you recall your armies after restoring the status quo, then the enemy is free to reinvade. To prevent that from happening, you have to leave your armies there.

And so, half a century later, an American army mandated by the United Nations remains in Korea.

Korea proved to be a frustration for the American public. There seemed to be no understanding of containment in reverse: of the wall that the adversary had erected around the Western world, and that Americans couldn't smash their way out of. It was what always stood between the United States and victory. Americans wanted to win and couldn't see why, in the modern world, their country wasn't allowed to win.

★   ★   ★

It happened again in Cuba, in the early 1960s.

In the Bay of Pigs fiasco of 1961, the United States unsuccessfully set about to overthrow the Communist dictatorship of Fidel Castro. In the missile crisis of 1962, the United States successfully persuaded the Soviet Union to remove its offensive missiles from Cuba.

Both episodes have been written about extensively. What is to be noted here is that once again the United States was contained by the adversary. For the relevant outcome was this: although Cuba is half a world away from Russia but only ninety miles from the coast of Florida, and therefore lies clearly within America's sphere, the Soviets effectively interposed themselves between the United States and Castro's island. Concluding the matter in 1962, the

United States promised not to invade Cuba again; and, surrendering the Monroe Doctrine, the United States agreed to the stationing of Soviet troops in Cuba, from which they could guard against the United States, even as American soldiers in South Korea guard against the North.

And then there was Vietnam. In the beginning—in 1963, 1964, and 1965—it was the contention of the Kennedy and Johnson administrations that what was happening was not a civil war in South Vietnam, but an invasion of the South by North Vietnam. They may well have been right. But they also understood, and continued to understand, that in order to prevent the war from widening, they could not invade North Vietnam. Yet it was from there that Communist forces in the South continued to replenish their supplies of men and equipment. A reason for extending immunity to North Vietnam was that if Americans invaded, the North Vietnamese, like the North Koreans before them, could count on an inexhaustible source of reinforcements from China. The United States therefore would have had to invade China, which was out of the question.

Putting aside (for they are not here relevant) all of the many other things that can be said about the Vietnam War, what should have been clear from the outset was that there was a line drawn around the American forces by the Soviet Union and China; that the United States could not win without stepping over that line; and that the United States could not step over the line without provoking a war against the Soviet Union and China—which America, wisely, would not do.

★   ★   ★

So long as the Communist powers balanced American power abroad, foreign interventions consistently failed to achieve the results for which Americans hoped. Not understanding the power constraints that were responsible, the public looked around for scapegoats; but whether one chose to blame the president, the military, or the media, the true causes remained unrecognized. European readjustments after World War I in large part were dictated by France, because it had the only major army remaining in the field, and global readjustments after World War II were dictated by Russia, because it had the only major army remaining in the field. However, large segments of American opinion, astonished and uncomprehending, could only imagine that the one was the work of a cabal of armaments manufacturers, and the other of Communist spies in the American government or of Franklin Roosevelt's personal failings at the Yalta Conference.

Looking back, we can see that power realities limited America's possibilities for achieving the results it desired in foreign affairs throughout the twentieth century. Looking at today and tomorrow, we have to ask ourselves what other constraints, perhaps less visible, have to be taken account of in making our plans from now on.

7

AMERICA UNBOUND

S TARTING IN 1989, Americans observed with wonder the ongoing dissolution of the Soviet Empire
and of the Soviet Union itself; the fall of Communist dictatorships behind what used to be, but no longer
was, the Iron Curtain; and the winding up of the Cold
War. These processes took about five years to achieve full
fruition, and at almost any given point along the way it remained unclear what the consequences of the continuing
drama were or would be for the United States and for the
rest of the world.

On August 2, 1990, when news reached President
George Bush that Iraq had invaded Kuwait, one of his first
thoughts, as he recalls, was "that this would be the first
post–Cold War test of the Security Council in crisis." He
allowed himself to hope that "our improving relations with
Moscow and our satisfactory ones with China offered the
possibility that we could get their cooperation in forging
international unity to oppose Iraq."

Bush knew that what he was going to ask the Soviet leaders to do "ran counter to Moscow's traditional interests and policy in the region." But his move to stop Iraq also would mean a turnabout in position for Washington. During the 1980–88 war between Iraq and Iran, both countries were enemies of the United States, so the longer they focused their attention and all their energies and resources on battling each other, the longer America might remain safe from their terrorist and other attacks. The United States thus tended to support Iraq as being the weaker party; aiding Baghdad would help prolong the fighting.

But somehow the American support for Iraq over the years developed a life of its own. Assessments of Iraqi dictator Saddam Hussein softened. His development of weapons of mass destruction somehow escaped scrutiny. His ambitions were seen to be more reasonable than they were in actuality. In 1989, the assistant secretary of state for Near Eastern and South Asian Affairs visited Baghdad and is quoted as having said, "You are a force for moderation in the region"—which a good diplomat would have said in any event, but which the State Department seems to have believed. Of Iraq's territorial and other demands on Kuwait, the U.S. ambassador told Saddam that it was a matter for Arabs to settle among themselves; America had no opinion.

When Iraq did invade and occupy Kuwait in August 1990, perhaps poising itself to invade Saudi Arabia as well, it turned out that the United States *did* have an opinion. President Bush spent a half year assembling a global military coalition to throw back the Iraqis. Freed from threat by the Communist world, America believed that at last it could act when and where it chose; and the United States–led coalition fought its campaign, Desert Storm, in the Persian Gulf War brilliantly, liberating Kuwait, expelling the Iraqi Army and chasing it back to Iraq itself—but then stopping.

Why had the American-led coalition gone to war against Iraq? Why had it stopped on the eve of victory? What were its objectives? What had it accomplished? These and other troubling questions surfaced even as the coalition forces celebrated and rejoiced. The Bush administration was tongue-tied all along in explaining to the public what it was doing—and why.

Obviously the country was not fighting to preserve American jobs (a bizarre explanation attributed to the secretary of state), nor was the United States acting to restore a constitutional democracy, for Kuwait was ruled, more or less arbitrarily, by a sheikh. The occupation of Kuwait did not threaten American oil supplies—Kuwait's oil mostly went to Japan—so that was not the explanation either.

Iraq is an artificial country, put together by Great Britain in the aftermath of World War I by joining together three former provinces of the Ottoman Empire. In the aftermath of the Gulf War, the joining together came undone: the Shi'ites of the south and the Kurds of the north made bids for freedom. It turned out that while the United States wanted to defeat Iraq and drive it from

Kuwait, it did not want the country to come apart; it believed it needed a strong Iraq to counter Iran. So the Shi'ites of the south were abandoned to Saddam, while the Kurds of the north were afforded protection only so long as they did not ask for independence.

It transpired that Washington believed that only a brutal dictator like Saddam could hold his country together and make it strong enough to act as a counterweight to Iran. But the administration did not want Iraq strong enough to threaten Western interests or local allies. The United States therefore was pursuing contradictory goals. Washington also wanted to destroy Iraq's arsenal of weapons of mass destruction, which perhaps was feasible; and to see Saddam killed and then replaced by someone just like himself, which was asking rather too much fine-tuning even of a Providence disposed to be friendly.

President Bush contributed to the confusion by using the language of Woodrow Wilson. According to Bush, what was being ushered in was a "new world order." Aggression had been repelled by an American-led coalition fighting under the auspices of an international institution: a league representing the countries of the planet.

But there remained one of the many weaknesses in the Wilson scheme: the aggressor that has been repelled can return to the attack as soon as the intervening army leaves. To deal with that, an American army had to be stationed permanently in the Gulf area, just as an American army continues to stand guard in Korea. And American aircraft were still attacking Iraqi radar in the spring of 1999 when beginning to fly similar sorties against Serbia in Kosovo. The Gulf War, like the Korean War, seems to be unending.

If it were true that the world now lived in a new order in which aggressions were repelled and atrocities prevented or punished, why didn't the United States liberate Tibet? Why didn't it stop the mass murder of the Tutsi in Rwanda in 1994 and 1995? Why be selective in doing good; why right some wrongs but not others?

A consideration of the American experience of intervening in Somalia may shed light on some of these questions.

★   ★   ★

Somalia is a country that occupies most of the Horn of Africa, at the northeast edge of the continent. To the north is the Gulf of Aden, and beyond that, the Arabian peninsula; to the east, the Indian Ocean. Somalia comprises a quarter million square miles, much of it desert, and has a population of 10 million. Until 1960 it was a trusteeship administered in part by Italy and in part by Britain.

Its longtime military dictator, Mohammed Siad Barre, fled the capital, Mogadishu, in January 1991, leaving Somalia a prey to widespread banditry, anarchy, and a civil war among a dozen or so factions. Drought struck as well, and at least a million and a half people faced starvation. In July 1992 the secretary-general of the United Nations called Somalia a country without a government.

Images of the starving population flashed across television screens in the Western world, and Americans were horrified by what they saw. Food supplies were sent to Somalia, but were intercepted by local warlords and never reached the mass of the inhabitants who were dying of hunger—on television, before the world's eyes.

In December 1992, in his last month in office, President Bush took action: he sent 28,000 troops to Somalia. The soldiers went there to make sure that the food got to the hungry. It was a purely humanitarian endeavor; the United States had no interests in Somalia. To foreign policy realists who argued that the United States should intervene abroad only in defense of the national interest, the administration replied that common humanity required that an exception be made in this case—and that the intervention was going to be *easy*. In effect the government was saying: "If we can't do it here, we can't do it anywhere." Expressing the consensus, *Newsweek* said it all: "Unlike the other charnel houses of the new world order, Somalia has no government to oppose intervention or allies to aid the resistance. It has no jungle, swamps or forested hills from which guerrillas can lash out at foreign intruders. It has no functioning air force and no real army, only ragtag gunmen who are far better at abusing helpless civilians than at standing up to determined invaders. Like the desert of Kuwait and Iraq, the hardscrabble Horn of Africa is a nearly ideal laboratory in which to test the theory that a high-minded application of force can right some of the world's wrongs."

Prudently, *Newsweek* added: "That doesn't mean the experiment will necessarily succeed."

★   ★   ★

At the outset, it *was* easy. The American troops, acting as part of a multinational force under the auspices of the United Nations, seized the key airstrips, ports, and cities. Logistical support by the United States allowed troops from thirty-two countries to assemble. The local warlords melted away. And then came the usual question: what next?

The United Nations put out feelers in the direction of trying to establish a viable government. This would have involved getting rival warlords to work together in the common interest. These were men who were deeply suspicious of one another, and with reason.

Mohammed Farah Aidid, a warlord and clan leader who had played a role in deposing Mohammed Siad Barre, came to believe that the United Nations aimed at squeezing him out of the government it was attempting to form. He struck back, ambushing and killing more than twenty Pakistani soldiers on June 5, 1993.

The United Nations proclaimed Aidid a criminal and put a price on his head. But he vanished into the surroundings and eluded capture in a five-month-long UN manhunt. It turned out that he was the most powerful of local warlords; a deal could not be made without him.

On August 8, four American soldiers were killed by land mines. On August 26, six others were wounded. Then, in October, U.S. forces were lured into an ambush at an urban hotel; first reports were that seventeen had been killed, seventy-seven wounded, one taken prisoner, and one unaccounted for.

When the pictures appeared on television of the American dead being dragged through the streets of Mogadishu, the U.S. public responded promptly, and the new president, Bill Clinton, reacted as the public did: the United States hastened to pull out.

On the first day of spring in 1994, after a frustrating mission that had lasted fifteen months, the last three thousand American troops sheltered themselves behind barbed wire in Mogadishu awaiting evacuation, while three miles away construction crews were preparing the ground for a gala homecoming celebration for Aidid: "a hero's welcome," as one of his supporters happily proclaimed.

★   ★   ★

One lesson of Somalia was that there is no such thing as a purely humanitarian intervention. A military intervention in a foreign country, unless undertaken at the request of its government, is political. It occurs because the United States, believing that the other country isn't being ruled properly, acts to overthrow the local leadership; but of course that obliges America to take over the government itself, and to remain there for the decades or centuries required to train the local population to elect proper rulers for themselves.

Military intervention also leads to fighting and in all likelihood to deaths. If Americans don't care enough about the country to die for it, then they shouldn't be there.

Somalia should have taught Americans, too, that invading, occupying, and administering a foreign country may not be as easy as it looks at first.

Above all, the lesson of Somalia was that, even in the absence of enemy great powers to restrain the United States, America is not completely free to make the world do as Americans wish. The constraints of reality may not be visible, but they are there.

Which brings us to Kosovo.

PART IV

ENTERING THE BALKAN MAZE

8

EAST AND WEST
SHAPE THE BALKANS

ROM TIME IMMEMORIAL the world has known that two of the peninsulas that border the Mediterranean and jut south from Europe into the sea—Iberia in the west and Italy in the center—define distinctive cultures. But only in the nineteenth century did Europeans recognize that the cluster of lands in the east of their continent, tending toward the Mediterranean and shooting out southward into the water, form a third to Iberia and Italy. Named "the Balkans" from a Turkish word that means forested mountains, its precise outlines are vague; it is more in the nature of a cultural entity than a geographical one. Its frontiers are uncertain, but a certain kind of politics has given the countries of the Balkans their distinctive character.

The Balkan states are Albania, Bulgaria, Greece, Romania (which often claims, with good geographic reason, not to be part of the peninsula), and the states into which the former Yugoslavia is now dividing itself: as of this writing, these are Bosnia-Herzegovina, Croatia, Macedonia, Serbia-Montenegro, and Slovenia, with the future of Kosovo (which lies within the borders of Serbia) at issue. In all, the Balkan states cover 320,000 square miles and have a population of about 65 million people.

The situation and physical features of the Balkans have played a large role in shaping their political culture. The peninsula adjoins the Middle Eastern Fertile Crescent and, with it, forms the crossroads of Africa, the Middle East, Asia, and Europe. From the days of the first humans, coming out of Africa and going to Europe and Asia, and until the last invasions of Europe by the nomadic Turks and Mongols in the fourteenth century, the peoples of the earth often have been in motion, with mass population migrations occurring from one region to another. Countless tribes and nations have passed through the Balkans on their way from one continent or river or sea to another; and some left legacies behind. Unlike Iberia and Italy, each sealed off on the north by forbidding mountain chains, the Balkans are easy of access. The territories to their north shade into the peninsula only gradually. Potential invaders find the way open.

Internally, however, the mountainous terrain keeps its diverse peoples isolated and apart: it works against unity. Cut off from one another in a mosaic of different communities, the inhabitants of the Balkans have retained their own religions, their own languages, their own style of dress, their own architecture, their own alphabets, and their own calendars.

To the outside world, the Balkan peninsula often has been pictured as a land that time forgot: of peasant villages from the Middle Ages; of feuds and clans, of conspiracies and assassinations. And Europe, in particular, remembers it—with reason—as a political labyrinth in which the great powers, if imprudent enough to enter it, can end up losing their way, or their lives.

★   ★   ★

A people called the Illyrians, speaking a language belonging to the Indo-European linguistic family, seem to have crossed from Asia Minor (today's Turkey) into the Balkans about 1000 B.C., at the end of the Bronze Age or the beginning of the Iron Age. Today's Albanians claim to be direct descendants of one of the tribes of these Illyrians. But the Serbs deny the Albanian claim.

Of the other early peoples of the Balkans, apart from the Greeks, we know little, except that they were various. When Philip of Macedon (today's Greek province of Macedonia) took possession of upper Macedonia (today's former Yugoslav republic of Macedonia) in the fourth century B.C., he ended up ruling subjects that were conspicuously diverse—so much so that in the modern world, restaurant chefs who cut up assorted fresh fruits into an assemblage of many tiny bits call it a *macédoine*.

Philip carved out for himself the earliest of Balkan empires. His son and successor Alexander, known to history as Alexander the Great, was obliged to put down revolts in the Balkans, from the Illyrians among others, and did so in order to restore his father's kingdom, before leading that kingdom in his successful quest to defeat Persia and to conquer the known world.

Some centuries after the Macedonian world empire rose and fell, the Balkans were brought into the orbit of the Roman Empire and of the Roman peace. It was a transforming experience to be governed by Rome, which had moved far along the road to achieving the unity of Mediterranean civilization. From Britain to what is now Iraq, and from the Sahara to the Rhine, a common culture prevailed. It did not entirely disappear even when the Roman Empire fell. The widespread culture became a legacy. Across the face of the Balkan peninsula today there still are, in beliefs and behavior, lines where the western empire stopped; the lines themselves are invisible, but it can be seen that on one side there was a Latin presence and that on the other side there was not.

But in the fourth century A.D. the Roman Empire, moving its capital eastward to Constantinople, began a transformation from one empire into two. Over the course of years, it moved steadily further in the direction of cutting itself in half: the Latin-speaking west and the Greek-speaking east.

It was in the west that Rome had become especially vulnerable, and it was there that the empire collapsed in the fifth century under the weight of invasions from the north by Germanic and other tribesmen. The city of Rome succumbed; but Constantinople, and its empire in

the wealthy Greek-speaking east, survived and ruled for a
thousand years more.

The split between western and eastern empires had begun as an administrative measure, but in time it became a
cultural one between Latin and Greek. The state religion,
Christianity, manifested a parallel break, between those
who looked for leadership to the bishop of Rome and
those who looked to the patriarch in Constantinople. In
1054, the split became final. From then on there were more
invisible lines through the Balkans dividing the Latin world
from the Greek world, and Roman Catholic from Greek
Orthodox.

★   ★   ★

The mass movement of barbarian tribes that had started
with the Huns riding west from the Chinese frontier, dis-
placing other tribes as they went, and that culminated in
the overthrow of the western empire in A.D. 476, continued to be a theme of the political and military life of Europe for the next one thousand years.

The most numerous of ethnic groups in Europe, the
Slavs, speakers of an Indo-European tongue, came long
before from Asia but had been in Europe for centuries before moving into the Balkans in about the sixth and sev-
enth centuries A.D. There they settled in lands nominally
falling under the sway of Byzantium: the eastern Roman
Empire centered in Constantinople. The Serbs, the Croats,
and the Slovenes were among the South Slavs that came to

the peninsula and eventually staked out claims to their respective Balkan domains.

In the ninth century, the Serbs accepted the Greek Orthodox faith, and ties between church and state became
close. By medieval times, much of the Serbian heartland
belonged to large monasteries. Serbia prospered, and by
the fourteenth century had become a great kingdom. The
center of that kingdom was Old Serbia, today called
Kosovo.

But trouble was gathering across the narrow bodies of
water in the southeast Balkans that separate Europe from
Asia. On the other side, the Asian shore, warrior bands had
been circling the Byzantine Empire, raiding and plunder-
ing, and establishing their own rule wherever they could.
Then they began crossing over to Europe, initially to serve
as mercenaries for local Christian rulers.

9

THE MIDDLE EAST
SHAPES THE BALKANS

URING THE FIVE CENTURIES that began in A.D.
1000, the main moving forces in Eurasian history
were the waves of invaders from the wastelands of
the East: the Turkish-speaking and Mongol nomads,
whose origins lay in the breeding grounds of horses and
warriors in the Asian steppe land east of the Caspian Sea.
The search for better pastures led them to leave their arid
fields, heading into China or the Middle East, where they
were attracted to the environs of civilization and to its
products. From city and town dwellers they obtained met-
als, textiles, and other goods they could not manufacture
for themselves. Some entered service as mercenaries. As a
result, those who rode west toward Byzantium, Asia Minor, and Europe were not entirely uncivilized.

Among the many Turkish-speaking central Asian warrior bands who emerged from a passage of perhaps centuries in the Middle East to battle their way to a position

on the frontiers of the eastern Roman Empire, history catches sight of the Ottomans in the thirteenth century. They had left the steppe in perhaps the ninth century; and despite their mixed ethnic origin, they had come to speak a common language. Originally followers of an animist religion, they, like other Turkish speakers who had spent time in the Middle East, had converted to the Sunni Muslim faith.

From Islam, they had taken the concept of the *ghazi:* the warrior for the Mohammedan religion in a holy war (a *jihad*). As a soldier of the faith, a *ghazi* led his war band in campaigns that were not merely raids conducted for plunder, but that had a spiritual dimension as well—to spread the faith.

Ancient tradition had it that the founding leader of this band was a certain Osman, whose followers therefore were called Osmanlis; and that "Ottoman" is explained as a corruption of "Osmanlis." At the end of the thirteenth century, the Ottoman Turks were established in their own emirate, on the Asian coast of the Sea of Marmora, just below Constantinople, and bordering on its defenses.

In the following century, the Ottomans went about creating a powerful state in Asia Minor, today's Turkey. From the start, fortune smiled upon them. The Turkish states to their south, potential rivals, ruined themselves in fighting one another, and also fell prey to invaders. To their north, the empire of Byzantium suffered one disaster after another, including the sack of Constantinople by Western European forces in the Fourth Crusade (1204) and the plague known as the Black Death (1340). As the Turkish state faced all that was left unconquered of wealthy Byzantium, with all the prospect for plunder such a situation implied, the Ottomans were able to attract adventurers from other freebooting bands.

By the middle of the fourteenth century, Ottoman forces had crossed over from Asia to Europe and had taken the city of Adrianople, which thereafter served as their base as they moved toward encircling Constantinople. From that and other key positions, they infiltrated Balkan territories that eastern Rome could no longer defend. They moved into Bulgaria and soon reached the Danube. They would next confront Serbia.

On the face of it, Serbia was the great power in the fourteenth-century Balkans. Once a client state of the Byzantine Empire, it aspired to take over from within much of Constantinople's authority. Its greatest ruler called himself Caesar—"Tsar"—and the official language of government was changed from Serbian to Greek as a further sign of its imperial character. Its territories now included much of what had been Byzantium's realm in the Balkans. Serbia seemed poised to capture Constantinople and replace Byzantium as the empire of the east.

But Serbia suffered from the Balkan disease: disunity. Its warrior lords were animated by ambitions of their own. Soon after the death of its Tsar in 1355, Serbia fell apart into separate principalities.

★   ★   ★

The most famous battle fought by medieval Serbia took place on the Field of the Blackbirds—*Kosovo Polje*—in 1389. Little is known of it that can be historically verified.

Nineteenth-century Serbian romance portrayed this as the decisive battle for control of the Balkans: the Ottoman Turks won it and the Serbs lost it, thereby destroying the Serbian state and condemning the region to suffer from Ottoman rule for the next five centuries. Historians tell us that while this story may be true in a metaphorical sense that is more important than mere facts, almost none of it is exactly accurate.

Under the respective commands of the Serbian prince Lazar and the Ottoman sultan Murad I, two armies did clash, but they were coalitions. Lazar's forces seem to have been mostly Serb, but probably included Hungarians and even Albanians. There were also some Serbs who fought on the Ottoman side.

The size of the opposing armies is unknown. Both the Serbs and the Turks claimed to have been outnumbered.

There is even a question whether the Turks won, though they were left in possession of the field of battle. It could have been a draw. Both sides suffered enormous losses, but these cannot be compared since the numbers are unknown. Both of the leaders, Lazar and Murad, were killed, though there are differing accounts of how and when Murad died. Lazar, as we recall from the gray falcon legend, had chosen in advance to die, in return for the promise of a heavenly kingdom.

Other battles are said by various historians to have been

more decisive in opening up the region to conquest, or in establishing Turkish overlordship in the Balkans, than was this first battle of Kosovo in 1389. Even more decisive, according to some, was the second battle of Kosovo in 1448 between the Ottoman Turks and the Hungarians, which confirmed the sultan's control of the Balkans.

The 1389 battle did not destroy the Serbian empire, which already had disintegrated, nor did it abolish the Serbian state, which continued to exist as an Ottoman vassal. Nor was resistance impossible afterwards, as witness the career of George Kastrioti ("Skanderbeg," 1405–1468), the Albanian warrior chief who repulsed more than a dozen Turkish invasions.

The great divide does not date from the loss of Kosovo in 1389, but from the fall of Constantinople in 1453. It was the Ottoman Empire that took the place of the Byzantine; and it did so with a surprisingly strong feel for the desirability of continuity.

★   ★   ★

For Rebecca West, as for any Victorian or Edwardian liberal, the thought of falling under Ottoman rule was equivalent to being plunged into darkness. It was a belief held without question. It was why West felt so strongly that instead of opting for a heavenly reward for losing at Kosovo, Prince Lazar should have fought to win. The consequence of losing—which was enduring Turkish rule for centuries—was too terrible for her to accept.

Not all historians today would wish to be associated with such sentiments. The more we learn of the Ottoman years, and the more we know of rule by other empires, the less, relatively speaking, we reproach the Turkish sultans. Indeed, in their time of glory in the fifteenth and sixteenth centuries, theirs was one of the high civilizations of the world.

Fernand Braudel, historian of the Mediterranean, tells us that the old order in the peninsula, to which the Ottomans brought an end, was not necessarily to be regretted. The pre-Ottoman Balkan world, he writes, "was extremely fragile—a mere house of cards. So it should not be forgotten that the Turkish conquest of the Balkans was assisted by an extraordinary social revolution. A seignorial society, exploiting the peasants, was surprised by the impact and collapsed of its own accord. The conquest, which meant the end of the great landowners, absolute rulers on their own estates, was in its way a liberation of the oppressed."

Above all, what the early sultans brought to the business of government was a certain amount of tolerance. Braudel writes that "Eventually Turkey created throughout the Balkans, structures within which the peoples of the Peninsula gradually found a place, collaborating with the conqueror and here and there curiously re-creating the patterns of the Byzantine Empire." The sultans did not deal with the religions, cultures, literatures, and customs of their new subjects as the conquistadors were to deal with those of the Indians of the New World. So long as the conquered peoples offered loyalty and tribute, their Ottoman rulers were content to live and let live.

If the peoples of the Balkans had causes to complain of Turkish rule—and they did—it was not during the vital couple of hundred years at the beginning, but only during the long centuries of decline that led to the empire's fall.

10

THE TWO HUNDRED
YEARS' CRISIS

FOR HUNDREDS OF YEARS the Ottoman Turks rode from conquest to conquest. It looked as though they could not be stopped, until they were. And once they were turned back on one front, it seemed as though they were being repulsed everywhere.

The traditional account is that Christendom was saved from the Turk in the late sixteenth century, in the course of a struggle for the island of Cyprus. At the time, Cyprus belonged to the Venetian Republic, the Ottoman Empire's chief rival for control of the eastern Mediterranean. Moving to invade Cyprus, the Turks assembled a vast armada. Venice obtained support from the Christian West; it won alliances with the pope and with the Habsburg Empire, then at its zenith. Under the command of Don John of Austria, an allied Christian fleet encountered and destroyed the Turks at the naval battle of Lepanto. It was fought on October 7, 1571, in the Gulf of Patras, off the western coast of Greece.

But tradition may overstate the decisiveness of the encounter. Soon afterwards, Venice ceded Cyprus to the Turks anyway, and the sultan rebuilt his fleet.

The furthest that Ottoman armies ever penetrated in their westward advance into Europe was Vienna. Twice they besieged the city. The first time, in 1529, the Turks broke off and went on to other conquests. The second time, in 1683, they mounted a siege of sixty days, but then withdrew to suffer one defeat after another.

It would be plausible to date the decline of the Turkish Empire from the second siege of Vienna, or perhaps from the subsequent Treaty of Carlowitz, signed on January 26, 1699. At Carlowitz, the Ottomans signed a peace treaty, perhaps for the first time, that they were forced to accept: the Christian victors dictated terms to the Muslim vanquished. The treaty transferred much of Hungary from Turkish to Austrian control. It was a major first step in rolling back the sultan's European empire.

The Ottoman power was kept on the defensive from then on. Prince Eugene of Savoy, commander of the forces of Habsburg Austria, routed Ottoman defenders of Belgrade in 1717 to capture the fortified city. Thereafter, Ottoman relations with Europe changed in a basic way.

The Sublime Porte—the gate to the grand vizier's offices in Constantinople from which the Ottoman government took its name—now recognized that to hold its empire, it would have to solicit the support of one or more European powers against the others. When threatened by Austria, the Ottoman Empire would call on France for aid.

And so it would go. Alliances and foreign policy would supply the security that Turkish armies by themselves no longer could assure.

The two European predators that pressed in on the Ottoman domains in the eighteenth century were Habsburg Austria, whose monarch was still known as the Holy Roman Emperor, and Imperial Russia, especially under the dynamic leadership of Catherine the Great (1729–1796). The Ottoman Turks continued to be on a losing streak. In almost every way, decay set in. Government, economy, and morale wound down.

By the nineteenth century, the Turkish Empire had become not so much a subject as an object of international politics. In its territories, rival European states vied for advantage; but the Porte was no longer a player on the world stage, having become instead merely a factor in the strategic designs of others.

It was taken as a given that its days, or at any rate its decades, were numbered. It was too vast for any one great power to annex, and it possessed too much of value for it to be divided among several of them, for greedy squabbling over the spoils would doom Europe to calamitous warfare.

For this reason, among others, Great Britain attempted to prop up the Ottoman Empire throughout the nineteenth century. It was a relatively consistent policy, departed from only during the Liberal government of William Gladstone in 1880–85; and among its chief objects was a desire to use the Ottoman Empire as a gigantic buffer between expansionist Russia in the north, and Britain's land and sea roads to India in the south.

★   ★   ★

"Turkey seems to be falling to pieces, the fall will be a great misfortune," Russian tsar Nicholas I told the British ambassador on January 8, 1853. "We have a sick man on our hands, a man gravely ill, it will be a great misfortune if one of these days he slips through our hands, especially before the necessary arrangements are made."

Thereafter, the sultan was known to those who interested themselves in foreign policy as "the Sick Man of Europe." For it was in respect of the Porte's European lands and peoples that the great powers felt a more or less urgent concern. It was the fate of Turkey-in-Europe that haunted nineteenth-century European diplomacy as "the Eastern Question." Only later did the phrase come to denote the issues raised by Turkey-in-Asia as well.

The Eastern Question aroused emotions because it was about Muslims ruling Christians and Asians ruling Europeans. It owed its immediacy to the surge of unrest within Balkan Turkey, at a time when the populations of other parts of the Ottoman domains remained relatively quiescent. Moreover, the Eastern Question brought into collision the vital interests and ambitions of the great powers, in particular pitting the two great multinational empires of Russia and Austria-Hungary against one another.

Turkey-in-Europe was in continuous ferment. The Ot-

toman regime was backward and corrupt, and lacked con-
viction. The best that could be said of it was that it was
usually ineffective. The various peoples of the Balkans
sought identity, and formed societies aimed at social and
cultural development and improvement. Nationalist com-
mittees were formed. Alliances and rivalries took shape.
There were revolts against economic feudalism. Most worrisome of all, the government provided no outlet for these
smoldering discontents, even though in Constantinople itself, the Porte did indeed launch a program aimed at reform and modernization: *at-Tanzimat,* or "re-ordering."

★   ★   ★

One by one, and later in concert with one another, the
European peoples of Turkey-in-Europe, Muslim and
Christian alike, tried to break away from the falling empire.

Croatia had been incorporated into Hungary nearly a
thousand years before and thus moved out of the Ottoman
orbit under the 1699 Treaty of Carlowitz; Slovenia had
been ruled by Germans of one sort or another for even
longer; both now were governed by Austria-Hungary. In
1815, Serbia won autonomy from the Turks, and maintained it, however precariously, with Russian diplomatic
support. In 1821, the Greeks rebelled against Turkish rule,
effectively winning independence in 1827 when a British-
French-Russian fleet commanded by a British admiral,
having been fired upon by the Ottoman fleet, responded
by sending the Turkish Navy to the bottom. These events

took place at a port called Navarino, on the southwest Greek coast. The Kingdom of Greece was created in 1832.

In the aftermath of the Crimean War (1853–56), in which Britain and France defeated Russia, Romania won unity and independence in 1861.

Revolts against Ottoman misrule broke out frequently in Bulgaria throughout the nineteenth century, for a variety of economic, political, religious, and nationalist reasons. In 1876, stretched thin, and lacking the regular troops to put down rebels, the Porte sent in "irregulars"—paramilitaries, we would say today—whose atrocities horrified even longtime British supporters of the Turkish regime. Outrage over the Bulgarian massacres helped to play a role in the British election results of 1880, when the Liberal William Gladstone turned the Conservative Benjamin Disraeli out of office, and then went on to sever Britain's informal alliance with Turkey.

Coinciding with the Bulgarian massacres of 1876 were revolutions against the empire in Bosnia-Herzegovina. Joining in, Serbia and Montenegro declared war on the Ottoman Empire. The Turks defeated the Serbs and their allies, but then, in 1877, Russia entered the fray, coming to the aid of its fellow Slavs. Russia defeated Turkey, and imposed severe terms on the Turks in 1878. The terms included the creation of an independent Greater Bulgaria that would have effectively become a Russian satellite.

The other great powers were alarmed at what appeared to be a Russian attempt to overthrow the existing balance of power in Europe. Britain and France had joined forces in the Crimean War to keep Russia from doing that before. In 1878, they banded together with the other great powers to do so again. Among the others were Germany and Austria-Hungary, who feared that Slavs might overwhelm Teutons in the Balkans.

At the Congress of Berlin in 1878 a new design for the Balkans was adopted by the European powers aligned against Russia. Although Albania and Macedonia were seething with nationalist unrest, they were to remain under Ottoman rule—though Macedonia was coveted by Bulgaria, Serbia, and Greece, all of them ready to fight for it. Bulgaria was confined to its northern part, and was returned to some sort of Turkish overlordship. Austria-Hungary was drawn further into the Balkans—a fateful error—by being awarded a mandate to administer Bosnia-Herzegovina under nominal Ottoman sovereignty. Britain was awarded the administration of Cyprus. Serbia graduated from autonomy to independence and the independence of neighboring Montenegro was confirmed as well.

The Congress had next to decide whether Turkey-in-Europe should continue to exist; and if not, what would replace it. The winner in Berlin was the Porte, as the Congress decided that Turkey-in-Europe should be preserved. The loser was the Russian tsar—and many of the peoples of the Balkans. The settlement aimed at restraining Russia rather than at satisfying the aspirations of the diverse peoples of the peninsula. Bulgaria would throw off Turkish suzerainty soon after, and Austria-Hungary would do the same in regard to Bosnia-Herzegovina in 1908; but condi-

tions in Ottoman Albania, Kosovo, and Macedonia remained chaotic. There was widespread dissatisfaction in
the region with the boundaries that had been drawn.

It would quickly become clear that the Congress of
Berlin had sown the seeds of disaster. Its Macedonian decision eventually led to the Balkan Wars of 1912 and 1913. Its
Bosnian decision led to the Great War that, with intermis-
sions, raged throughout almost all of the twentieth century, ending only with the Cold War's last gasp in 1994.

It was not a good portent for foreign great powers de-
sirous of imposing their own idea of a settlement in the
Balkans.

11

THE BALKAN WARS ERUPT

EVEN AS EUROPE entered the twentieth century, the Ottoman Empire visibly did not. It was an anachronism, a holdover from some bygone age, like the shattered ancient cities of classical antiquity that dotted its coastline, half buried by the sands of time. It was more relic than reality, and its landscape was that of the past. It lived without electricity or telephones. The streets of its cities were unpaved. Its peoples wore the fez, the veil, and an assortment of traditional garments that tourists found colorful and picturesque because they were so backward.

The empire did not cohere. Its government leaders in Constantinople, who came from generations of *ghazi* war bands of mixed origin, all spoke Turkish, but did not form an ethnic group. Many were the descendants of formerly Christian Balkan peoples who had converted to Islam to join the warrior class. Nor was the population as a whole an ethnic group. There was no Ottoman people. Indeed, the concept of nationality was an alien one, held by some of the captive European peoples, but not by the Turkish-speaking warriors of mixed blood who had conquered them.

Religion was the principle of alignment and loyalty, along with family and tribe or town. Language was less important. Perhaps half of the empire's subjects, at least in the Middle East, spoke Arabic rather than Turkish.

The empire was a theocracy, a Muslim state, and the sultan was a caliph, a Muslim leader. A large percentage of the population was Muslim, too. But even this did not guarantee real coherence. Though the sultans, as Sunnis, belonged to the majority group in the Mohammedan world, theirs was only one of the seventy-one sects into which Islam was divided.

Within the Muslim Empire, Christians and Jews, recognized as "peoples of the book," lived their own lives, tolerated but less privileged. They had their own "millets," communities that enjoyed autonomy in such matters as marriage and divorce.

Depending on who was doing the counting, the empire governed somewhere between twenty-three and thirty-six different peoples, and it made no effort to amalgamate them, to build a nation to support the state. In the feebleness that had overtaken it, the Ottoman Empire preferred to rule by dividing its subjects against one another rather than by uniting them.

It had taken on too much; it had taken too many into its fold. After a heroic nineteenth-century effort to reform itself through its "re-ordering" movement, the Porte gave up on modernizing. It was tired. Its ramshackle administration was incapable of collecting taxes, or of stamping out the brigandage that was prevalent throughout vast territories nominally under Ottoman rule.

Under the despotic rule of Sultan Abdul Hamid, who reigned from 1876 to 1909, the constitution was suspended, parliament was disbanded, Christians at times were massacred, political activity was suppressed, and a secret police force kept control of the capital city and its environs. Opposition, which had become illegal, therefore centered on societies that had to be kept secret; and those secret societies that were best placed to act were those formed in the army.

★   ★   ★

The focal point of opposition to the sultan was in the Balkans, and in particular Macedonia. It was a frontier posting for the Ottoman troops sent there and had something of the lawlessness of the American Wild West about it. Intrigue was rife among the soldiery. The Committee of Union and Progress (CUP), or Young Turkey Party, was a secret society that counted ambitious army officers among its members; and it sparked a revolt in 1908, based in Salonika, a city said by the enemies of the CUP to be filled with freethinkers, Freemasons, and Jews.

The 1908 revolt brought promises of reform from the Porte, promises that were not redeemed in the five years of turmoil that followed. But the CUP was making promises as well, promises of secularization and modernization and that all the peoples of the Ottoman Empire would have full participation in its affairs.

Albanians in what today is Albania and Kosovo believed in the promises, and in 1908 they rose in support of the Young Turks. For more than a quarter of a century they had feared that, because most of them were Muslim, they would find their lands taken from them if Christian Europe were to impose a new order in the Balkans. Many Albanians asked for autonomy within the empire, but generally supported the Porte against its enemies.

Also in 1908, Austria-Hungary discarded its mandate from the Congress of Berlin and formally annexed Bosnia-Herzegovina. This set off six turbulent years in which history moved at an accelerated rate. The sequence of events is so difficult to follow that it can seem dizzying. What was happening, in short, was the dissolution of the Ottoman Empire in Europe. The Eastern Question at last was being resolved, but in perhaps the worst possible way. As European diplomats had feared all along, the great powers allowed themselves and their interests to be implicated in it. For Germany it was merely the occasion, but for Russia and Austria it was the cause, of the explosion that followed.

★   ★   ★

In 1909, the CUP threw its support behind a program to consolidate the empire by "Ottomanizing" it. This broke its promises to the Albanians, who revolted in 1910. The revolt is said to have persuaded the CUP that it would be impossible to get the various peoples of the empire to unify. The Young Turks were about to crush the Albanians when Montenegro, planning to take Albanian lands for itself, attacked the Turks. Given a respite, Albanians were able to rise again in 1911. Hostilities ceased temporarily when the Porte made promises of autonomy.

Italy was encouraged by the Albanian rebellion to indulge its dreams of empire. Alone among the great powers, it did not own colonies, and it coveted them. Believing that the Ottoman Empire was distracted by the Albanian insurrection, Italy declared war in 1911. The Italians invaded the Ottoman province of Libya in North Africa and occupied the Dodecanese Islands in the Aegean Sea. In 1912, the Porte in effect accepted defeat: Italy took Libya, and promised to give back the Dodecanese but did not do so.

That same year, Albania revolted again and seized Skopje, the capital of Macedonia. How the Albanian-Turkish war would have been settled is something that never will be known, for the war was suspended while the Ottoman Empire dealt with another attack, in what has come to be known as the First Balkan War.

Temporarily putting aside their rival ambitions, the Christian states of the peninsula—Serbia, Bulgaria, Greece, and Macedonia—formed a Balkan League that essentially drove the Ottoman Empire out of Europe in 1912. At the end of the year Serbia captured and annexed Kosovo, Old Serbia, the onetime heartland of the state, in which stood the monuments of Serbia's medieval glory, but which for centuries (somewhere between two and twenty, depending upon which version you accept, but probably closer to two) had been inhabited mostly by Albanians.

During the war Albania declared independence, and the great powers, seeking to impose a solution, backed the declaration. The powers forced Serbia to give back some Albanian land taken in the fighting. For doing so, Serbia demanded compensation from its allies, insisting that they share some of what they had taken for themselves. Disputes ensued.

The Porte was devastated by the loss of its European empire. Blaming the old established figures for the defeat, the Young Turks seized power in a coup d'état in which their most charismatic leader, Enver Pasha, gave himself a military command.

But the Balkan allies had undergone a falling out over the spoils of victory. Bulgaria, which had played the leading role in defeating Turkey, felt especially aggrieved because it believed itself entitled to all of Macedonia, but instead was obliged to share it with Serbia and Greece.

In the summer of 1913, Bulgaria launched a surprise attack on its erstwhile allies, Serbia and Greece, with the aim of seizing Macedonia for itself. Montenegro then joined the allies, as did Romania, which had not previously been involved. The four countries defeated Bulgaria, and deprived it of much of its share of the winnings in Macedonia from the 1912 war.

While the Balkan countries were distracted by their disputes, Enver Pasha led the Ottoman forces in retaking the key city of Adrianople on the European side. But more bloodshed was to come.

★   ★   ★

Members of the Serbian government turned to the planning of an event that might shake the hold of Austria-Hungary on Bosnia-Herzegovina, the former Ottoman province that the Serbs regarded as part of their rightful patrimony. It was a plan to attack the heir to the Habsburg throne, the Archduke Franz Ferdinand, as he, his wife, and their entourage visited the Bosnian capital of Sarajevo—as it happened, on the anniversary of the battle of Kosovo.

On June 28, 1914, the attack was made, and due to a series of improbable accidents, the archduke and his consort were assassinated. Austria demanded what amounted to a surrender by Serbia of its independence. Serbia refused, with Russia coming to Serbia's support. Germany demanded that Russia back down. Russia refused. Germany declared war, and launched an invasion of France because the French were allied to Russia. The German invasion of France took place through Belgium, the neutrality of which England long ago had guaranteed; so Great Britain declared war on Germany. This chain of events may not have been as mindless, programmed, and automatic as it sounds. The army chief of staff in Austria-Hungary had been looking for a chance to smash Serbia and the army chief of staff in Germany had been waiting for a chance to attack Russia, while England's chief of staff had made plans, if war came, to aid France.

A few months later, for reasons of its own, the Ottoman Empire enlisted in the war on the German side, allied with the kaiser and the Habsburg emperor against Britain, France, Russia, and Serbia.

The Third Balkan War had begun, and it engulfed the entire world, becoming the Great War, from which the twentieth century has only just recovered.

In the beginning of the war, Greece, Romania, and Bulgaria remained neutral, though all would join in later. Albania dissolved into chaos. The Ghegs of the north and the Tosks of the south, Christians and Muslims, Sunnis and rival Muslims, clans and brigands, drifted apart, some choosing sides in the war and others not. The great powers had sent out a German prince and proposed that he become Albania's monarch; but after a stay of six months, he left the country to enlist in the German Army.

Serbia repulsed the Habsburg invaders decisively, but later was crushed when the armies of Germany and Bulgaria joined those of Austria-Hungary, and in effect was erased from the political map. The Serbian government and what remained of its armies escaped, marching in wintertime through narrow mountain passes to the Adriatic coast, where they were evacuated to Corfu to spend much of the war in exile. The Serbs returned in time to fight in the war's final rounds.

Everyone looked forward, whether with hope or foreboding, to the eventual victory in which the new masters of the world, whoever they might turn out to be, would redraw all the maps.

PART V

THE MAKING OF THE

MODERN BALKANS

12

REDRAWING THE MAP
AND STARTING OVER

THE GREAT WAR, as people once called the 1914–18 conflagration, was a gigantic and terrible act of creative destruction. It was like a raging fire that, by razing a metropolitan center to the ground, clears the way to build a new city. It leveled a civilization that then was rebuilt on new foundations. From World War I came the twentieth century.

The horse-drawn, candlelit world of 1914, in which the three great dynastic multinational empires clashed by night for overlordship of the Balkan peninsula, is gone forever, along with its archdukes and countesses. The Balkans that emerged from the peace conferences at Paris in 1919–20 are the Balkans that we have known ever since. The principles at stake in the Yugoslav politics of 1999, going forward into the twenty-first century, are those that were developed and applied by the peacemakers at Paris in their deliberations in 1919. The positions taken by President Clinton in the 1990s are those staked out for the United

States by President Wilson eighty years ago, when the century was young.

★   ★   ★

On December 18, 1917, Woodrow Wilson dined and conferred at the White House with his intimate adviser and alter ego, Edward House. House had just returned from wartime Europe, where he had met, as the president's representative, with the Allied leaders. He had come back to the United States to report their concerns, and his own.

The Colonel (it was a merely honorary title, but House used it all the time) was worried that the public on the Allied side might begin to believe that the war was being prolonged in the pursuit of imperialist gains by Great Britain and France. It was well known that the Allies coveted territorial gains in Africa, the Middle East, and elsewhere. At the same time, according to the Allies, the peoples of the enemy Central Powers, Germany and Austria-Hungary, might have come to suspect that it was *their* leaders who were continuing the war in search of empire; and such suspicions, House agreed, should be exploited. Above all, House and the Allies saw an urgent need to appeal to the peoples of Russia to stay in the war despite what their new government, Lenin's revolutionary Bolshevik regime, was telling them about the Allies being no better than their enemies.

To meet all three concerns, House proposed that the president should make a public statement of the enlightened war goals for which the United States was fighting.

According to House, he and Wilson discussed the matter for no more than ten or fifteen minutes. They needed no more, for they found themselves in complete agreement.

Wilson asked House to supply him with a memorandum that outlined the issues that could be expected to come up at the peace conference. He wanted the memo to be obtained from the Inquiry, a group of scholars and experts that had been assembled secretly in New York by House, at Wilson's request, to prepare position papers independently of the State Department.

House was given two versions of a memo by Walter Lippmann, who had drafted them on behalf of himself and two other members of the Inquiry team. Neither memo was entirely on point, because House had not been at liberty to disclose what use he and Wilson were going to make of the memos.

Late in the evening of January 4, 1918, House returned to the White House, and he and the president went to work on formulating America's goals. At times they worked together; at other times, Wilson worked alone. House later claimed that it was his idea to number the various goals.

As their first six points, the two friends listed broad general principles in which the United States believed, such as disarmament and open diplomacy. These were goals sought by the United States on behalf of all the countries of the world, itself included. These six points originated with Wilson and House, and had not been suggested by the Inquiry.

Their next seven points dealt with the claims and conflicts of other countries involved in the war, and as a reminder of the matters to be covered, Wilson used a Lippmann memo outlining what the various belligerents might expect from a peace agreement. Wilson decided to use the word "should" rather than "must" for these seven points, because they dealt with quarrels to which the United States was not a party—was no more than a spectator, in fact—and thus in which he had done no more, in his points, than spell out what a disinterested America regarded as fair solutions. They were not terms that the United States was demanding, either for itself or for the world.

The last point, numbered 14, was a "must" rather than a "should." It proclaimed—on everybody's behalf—the need for a postwar League of Nations to keep the peace.

Wilson incorporated his Fourteen Points in a message to Congress two weeks later, on January 18, 1918, and they took the world by storm. They made the United States seem entirely unselfish; of its war goals, not one seemed to serve a purely national interest.

Encouraged, Wilson went on to amplify his statements of American principles as they applied to the coming peace in his Four Principles, Four Ends, and Five Particulars—all of them public statements issued in 1918.

Walter Lippmann assumed that these statements had been approved, or at least cleared, in advance by the Allies. They had not been. In the autumn of 1918, when the Central Powers sought to surrender on the basis of the Fourteen Points, the Allies refused to accept their offers until the points were redefined and narrowed (as they then were, by Lippmann and another journalist, Frank Cobb, under the supervision of House). The defeated powers were not informed that the Fourteen Points agreed to by the Allies in regard to the German surrender were not identical to the Fourteen Points on the basis of which they sought to end the war.

* * *

In the summer of 1918, the Central Powers lost their ability to continue fighting. The Austro-Hungarian Army was disintegrating from within, as its diverse nationalities fell apart, while the German Army reeled under blows on the western front. As *The First World War: Germany and Austria-Hungary 1914–1918,* a recently published study of these events by Holger H. Herwig, makes clear, "The home front likewise had collapsed. Workers and veterans, women and children went about in rags, adult skeletons rummaging through garbage heaps to glean pieces of rotten meat, congealed blood, and decayed vegetables. The Allies estimated late in 1918 that an adult required at least 2500 calories per day to work; German labourers were down to 1000 calories. . . . More than 250,000 Germans had died of malnutrition in 1918 alone. In Austria-Hungary both the food supply and the transportation system had collapsed totally."

In the Balkans, a lightning French-led Allied strike from Salonika knocked Bulgaria out of the war; and because of Bulgaria's key geographical position, Germany, Ottoman Turkey, and what had been the Habsburg Empire sued for peace.

But events moved too fast. The Habsburg emperor disappeared; Hungary separated from Austria; Croatia seceded from Hungary; in Germany, Austria, Hungary, and even the Ottoman Empire, leaders fled to safety and there seemed to be no government willing and able to take charge in order to surrender. The myriad peoples of the Balkans moved out of the political structures in which they had lived for centuries, as those structures collapsed.

By November 13, when an independent Hungary signed an armistice in Belgrade, cease-fires were in place in the Balkans, but disorder reigned. It now remained only to make peace.

13

WILSON'S PRINCIPLES IN ACTION

NO AMERICAN PRESIDENT had gone overseas during his term of office, but Wilson, breaking with precedent, did so. He was determined to head the American delegation and to supervise the peace negotiations personally. He argued that the peace should be based on the principles of justice that he had espoused in his public statements throughout 1918.

He sailed from the New World to Europe on the ship *George Washington,* which docked at Brest on the French coast on Friday, December 13, 1918. He traveled for several weeks before the Paris Peace Conference began in mid-January 1919. He was greeted in Europe as nobody had been before. In Paris, hundreds of thousands of Frenchmen took to the streets crying, "Wil-son! Vive Wil-son!" It was the same everywhere.

The conference began amidst confusion and delirium. More than a thousand Americans had come. Perhaps ten

thousand people arrived from all over the world to participate in the proceedings. Armenia alone was represented by
forty-two rival delegations.

A shadow was cast over the opening sessions by the
news that armed forces of one sort or another were on the
move throughout anarchic Central and Eastern Europe.
Champions of various causes were attempting to create
faits accomplis that would preempt the rights of the peace
conference to make decisions about national borders.

Wilson asked and received the consent of the Allies on
January 24 to telegraph and publish all the world over the
following statement: "The governments now associated in
conference to effect a lasting peace among the nations are
deeply disturbed by the news which comes to them of the
many instances in which armed force is being made use of,
in many parts of Europe and the East, to gain possession of
territory, the rightful claim to which the Peace Conference is
going to be asked to determine. They deem it their duty to
utter a solemn warning that possession gained by force will
seriously prejudice the claims of those who use such means."

★   ★   ★

Which countries at the peace conference would have a say
in the decisions about to be made? At the start, the defeated enemy states were excluded, and they never were
permitted to attend; at the end it became plain that the
peace terms would be dictated to them. Nothing was asked

of them—or permitted to them—but to sign the documents placed in front of them.

Nor were most of the other countries to do much more. The Paris Peace Conference turned into a summit meeting of the great powers. At first they met as the Ten, with two delegates from five powers; and then, at one time or another, as the Five, the Four, the Three, or the Two. France and Great Britain always were numbered among them. The United States, Italy, and sometimes Japan were the others.

The conference, as it turned out, did not deal with the enemy states as a group. Instead, it dealt with each one separately. A treaty was prepared with Germany first, and was signed in the early summer of 1919. Treaties were then prepared and presented to Austria, Hungary, Bulgaria, and Turkey for signature later.

But this schedule was not known in advance. Indeed, when the Supreme Council of the Allied and Associated Powers assembled for the first time in Paris in January 1919, it became evident that there was no agreed-upon agenda. This omission was all the more important because there was a radical split on priorities.

On December 14, 1918, Wilson had explained to House that the creation of a League of Nations was the center of his entire program for the Paris settlement. In the nature of things, it had to come first. As Wilson saw it, the League would be like a court of appeals that could change any of the specific decisions arrived at in Paris. With the League in place, it would not matter so much how quarrels among the Allies were resolved at the conference: in the end, justice would prevail.

Georges Clemenceau, the French premier, put national security first. He told the Chamber of Deputies on December 29 that he believed in alliances. What he proposed to do at the conference was to forge a permanent military alliance among the three major victors—Britain, the United States, and France—aimed at keeping Germany down. The alliance would be dedicated to the enforcement and perpetuation of the treaty of surrender that would be forced upon the Germans.

To Clemenceau, the League seemed meaningless. Since it was meaningless, it was, in the Frenchman's view, harmless; and in a gesture of generosity, he allowed Wilson to go ahead and obtain approval from the conference of his proposed League before the peacemakers went on to more vital matters.

The League was intended to prevent warfare. That was what its proponents in Britain and the United States claimed that it would do. Wilson had persuaded his followers that the conflict in which they had been engaged was a war to end all wars. Now, in the time of victory, Wilson presented his plan to accomplish his goal of abolishing warfare.

The heart of his program was article 10 of the Covenant of the League. It pledged states to respect the existence and frontiers of other states, and not to try to alter either by force: which is to say, by aggression. The pledge extended only to fellow members of the League. But enthusiasts for the Covenant envisaged a time when all states of the world would belong to the League. The plan, therefore, was to freeze the political structure of the world as of 1919. As states rarely give up either their existence or their frontiers except when forced to do so, and as the use of force was being outlawed, the League was supposed to put an end to structural changes in international politics.

It was a program that the American people believed in. This would be reaffirmed in the Kellogg-Briand Pact of 1927–28 renouncing war, and in the Charter of the United Nations, which forbids not only the use but also the threat of force.

The history of the United States showed that Americans went even further: in their view, not merely should map changes not be made by arms, by external forces, neither should they be made by internal ones. In 1861, the federal government refused to allow the southern states to secede. Americans proposed to put a stop to secessions as well as to aggressions. This would set the tone for much of U.S. foreign policy in the century to come.

★   ★   ★

Wilson already had applied these principles to the question of the postwar Balkans. It was one of the issues that he had dealt with in his Fourteen Points. Lippmann and his colleagues, whose memo the president had in hand as he drafted his points, had expressed a willingness to discuss the possible breakup of the Habsburg Empire, but Wilson drew back from that, suspecting that the Habsburgs still had a role to play in providing stability for the region. He therefore preferred to keep the empire intact while providing legal rights for the various nationalities it ruled. In its final form, the tenth of Wilson's points read: "The peoples of Austria-Hungary, whose place among the nations we wish to see safeguarded and assured, should be accorded the freest opportunity of autonomous development."

The twelfth of the points proposed much the same for the peoples of the Ottoman Empire: the Turks should remain independent, while the other peoples were to enjoy only "autonomous development."

Another of Wilson's points proposed to protect the integrity of the existing states of Serbia, Montenegro, and Romania, which had fought on the Allied side, and suggested in vague language the structure of their future relations along "established" lines.

Wilson was proposing to prop up the existing imperial structures, while creating new legal protections in the form of a defined autonomy for the peoples they governed.

★   ★   ★

Events overtook Wilson's program. The three great dynastic multinational regimes that ruled so much of Europe came apart. The empire of the Romanovs had collapsed in early 1917; that of the Habsburgs in late 1918; while that of the Ottomans suffered a lingering death between 1918 and 1922.

The nationalities issue had surfaced long before in the European domains of all three. It was the issue that, at Sarajevo in 1914, had sparked the war. It was felt passionately.

The slogan of "self-determination" seems to have blown in from the propaganda wars in 1917. Wilson either picked it up or invented it soon after. In 1918, the phrase was used by the American president in two speeches to Congress, the first time in quotes, as a neologism, but only months later without quotation marks, so rapidly had it entered the common parlance of politics.

"'Self-determination' is not a mere phrase," Wilson told Congress, "it is an imperative principle of action which statesmen will henceforth ignore at their peril." Later he referred to "the free self-determination of nations upon which all the modern world insists."

Certainly, self-determination seemed to flow from the principle of government only with the consent of the governed, a fundamental principle for Americans, often articulated by Wilson. Yet it comes into conflict with the new American principle that war must not be allowed to upset the status quo and bring about armed conflict. Wilson's own secretary of state, Robert Lansing, was deeply concerned about the implications if this concept were to be implemented on a broad scale. "The phrase," he wrote, "is simply loaded with dynamite. It will raise hopes which can never be realized. It will, I fear, cost thousands of lives."

Addressing Congress again, Wilson defined his position more fully. Recognizing the dangers that the principle of self-determination might pose for Europe, he cautioned the Congress (in the fourth of his Four Principles, on February 11, 1918) that "all well defined national aspirations shall be accorded the utmost satisfaction that can be accorded them *without introducing new or perpetuating old elements of discord and antagonism that would be likely in time to break the peace of Europe and consequently of the world*" (emphasis added).

But of course that is what self-determination does. It does bring discord. It does upset the peace.

The question arose for Wilson in concrete form with regard to Austria-Hungary.

★   ★   ★

The program of uniting the three southern Slav peoples had been inspired by Josip Strossmayer (1815–1905), a Croat leader and Roman Catholic bishop. He worked for a federation of Serbs, Croats, and Slovenes; and also for the union of Roman Catholic and Greek Orthodox churches. Over the years, his ideas won converts.

From Corfu, where the Serbian government and army remained in exile, there had issued on July 20, 1917, a Declaration by the prime minister of Serbia and other South Slav leaders affirming the ideal of a unified state of Serbs, Croats, and Slovenes, to achieve independence after the war as a constitutional, democratic, and parliamentary monarchy under the royal house of Serbia. The Declaration of Corfu claimed the right of the three South Slav peoples to self-determination.

It was a victory for the regent, Prince (later King) Alexander, who had espoused the Yugoslav dream. Uniting with Croats and Slovenes would give him expanded horizons for leadership. The prime minister had resisted as he did not want to have to share rule with non-Serbs.

The Yugoslav cause owed much to the sympathetic support given it by Thomas Masaryk (1850–1937) as he advanced his own cause, that of Czechoslovakia, to be carved out of three Slavic northern provinces of the Habsburg Empire. Masaryk was a towering figure, who had inspired support for the Allied cause throughout Central Europe. In the spring of 1918, Masaryk visited Washington to negotiate with the American government. He secured U.S. support for the creation both of a Czechoslovakia and a Yugoslavia in the form of an official statement of sympathy for these causes by the secretary of state: the Lansing Declaration of May 29, 1918. On June 3, Czechoslovakia was recognized as an Allied power.

So within six months of having expressed support for retaining Austria-Hungary as is, the president had committed himself to its destruction, and to radical reconstruction in the form of creating two new Slav federations.

On October 4, 1918, when Austria-Hungary asked the United States to be allowed to surrender on the basis of Wilson's Fourteen Points, Washington had to reply that it was no longer possible because the United States had changed its position by recognizing Czechoslovakia and Yugoslavia as belligerents on the Allied side.

★   ★   ★

Writing in 1944, a quarter century later, Walter Lippmann, who had been as close to the situation as anyone then still alive, asserted that although Wilson eventually decided to break up the Austro-Hungarian Empire, and at the time did invoke the principle of self-determination, "he did not believe in it"—not even then.

"To invoke the general principle of self-determination, and to make it a supreme law of international life," wrote Lippmann in *U.S. War Aims,* is "to invite sheer anarchy. For the principle can be used to promote the dismemberment of practically every organized state."

Having abandoned his principle of the integrity of existing states, the entire basis of his system for outlawing war, and having forsaken it for the principle of self-determination, the president when in Paris was faced with the logical consequences: it seemed as though everyone claimed to be entitled to have a state of their own.

According to Colonel House, Wilson's pledge of self-determination "brought to Paris many and diverse delegations from Europe, Asia, and Africa. They were the most picturesque as well as the most ill-informed and unreasoning of all those who gathered around the historic centre where the peace was made."

Wilson complained to the Senate Committee on Foreign Relations in 1919 that "When I gave utterance to those words ('that all nations had a right to self-determination') I said them without the knowledge that nationalities existed, which are coming to us day after day. . . . You do not know and cannot appreciate the anxieties that I have experienced as the result of many millions of people having their hopes raised by what I have said."

The president gamely tried to retrieve the situation. He told the Senate that he had been misunderstood. He had never intended to reopen questions that had been settled, rightly or wrongly, long ago. He had not meant "to inquire into ancient wrongs." And his new principle of self-determination only should operate within narrow bounds. It would not apply, he said, to prewar treaties; and it would apply only to the territory of powers defeated in the 1914–18 war.

The United States now had three principles in international politics that did not quite fit with one another. Americans believed in the sanctity of existing states and frontiers; in the legal protection of minorities within those states ("human rights," though at that time focused on groups rather than individuals); and in the right of nations to break up states in the name of self-determination—sometimes.

Resolving these inherent contradictions would not prove easy for future American leaders.

14

THE BALKAN PEACE
SETTLEMENT OF 1920

O N JUNE 28, 1919, the anniversary of the first
battle of Kosovo and, more to the point, five
years to the day since the assassination at Sarajevo, Germany signed a peace treaty with the Allies at Versailles. The United States signed, but later did not ratify,
the treaty; America made its separate peace in the Treaty of
Berlin of August 25, 1921.

From the summer of 1919 to that of 1920, the Allies
worked on the drafting of treaties with the other defeated
powers. They worked in Paris, and arranged signings of
each treaty in one or another suburb of the city. Wilson
had gone home in July 1919, but Americans were still stationed in the French capital, under orders from their departed president to do nothing and make no decisions until
they heard further from him.

Back in the United States, the Versailles treaty, and the
Covenant of the League of Nations that was incorporated
in it, fell victim to the rancorous personal and political feud

between Wilson and the Republican Senate leader Henry Cabot Lodge. More than two-thirds of the Senate and about 80 percent of the country were in favor of ratification, but Lodge would allow it only with his proposed reservations, requiring congressional approval before the United States would be bound by major League decisions. Wilson, however, would allow ratification only without Lodge's reservations. The result was stalemate.

Barnstorming around the country on behalf of his own program, Wilson collapsed, apparently from a stroke. He was brought back to the White House, where he and his presidency lay paralyzed. He became incommunicado: his wife would not allow communications to get through to him. The cause of American entry into the League of Nations was lost.

★   ★   ★

It was without the Americans, therefore, that the peacemakers in Paris continued work on the fate of the peoples who had lived under the rule of the multinational empires in Europe, and on the fate of their onetime rulers.

The case of Austria came first. It was, in terms of formalities, immensely complicated. The territory had been part of a dynastic domain and not a state in its own right. It was one of the territories belonging to the Habsburg family, and it was the Habsburg regime that, under the arcane rules of public international law, enjoyed international recognition. And the last emperor, though he renounced all share in government and fled, did not abdicate.

The Allies made the fundamental decision that German Austria—which is to say, the German-speaking section of the Habsburg Empire—should stand alone as an independent country. It would not be, nor would it ever be allowed to become, a part of Germany. Nor would it remain joined to any of the other lands the Habsburgs had ruled.

A government was found for the new country, which was recognized by the Allies. A national assembly elected the Social Democratic leader Karl Renner to be chancellor, and to head the Austrian delegation to Paris. At 7:00 p.m. on May 12, 1919, Renner and his delegation boarded a train in Vienna. Nearly forty-eight hours later, at 6:00 p.m., May 14, they arrived at Saint-Germain-en-Laye, forested former hunting grounds twenty-one kilometers outside Paris, where they were greeted by the local prefect. They were then shown to their quarters in nearby villas, and told to wait.

They waited four months. Then they were given a treaty to sign, modeled, as all treaties were to be, on that of Versailles, and beginning with the Covenant of the League of Nations. The Treaty of St. Germain provided for large-scale changes in the map, without resort to plebiscites. Austria was left with about a quarter of the "Austria" that had formed half of the Habsburg state.

Hungary, Austria's partner at the head of the Dual Monarchy, fared badly as well. During the spring and summer of 1919, Hungary was in the midst of a governmental crisis, with the Communists (under the charismatic leadership of Bela Kun) having seized power, only to be driven out a few months later. It was thus not until June 4, 1920, that its peace treaty, named after the Trianon at Versailles, was ready to be signed. Like Austria, Hungary too was to be cut off from the other Habsburg lands, which in terms of square miles lost made it the biggest loser among the defeated powers, giving up two-thirds of its prewar territory in the Treaty of Trianon.

The subject peoples of the Austro-Hungarian Empire found their lands divided primarily among three new states: Poland (which also gained territory from Germany and Russia) in the east, Czechoslovakia in the north, and the Kingdom of the Serbs, Croats, and Slovenes in the south. Ten years later, in 1929, this last country would adopt a new name—Yugoslavia.

The new world created by the Allies in Central and Eastern Europe was in many ways like the old. Many frontiers had been redrawn, and territories had changed hands; but self-determination remained thwarted. As in the prewar world, there were "peoples of state": the Czechs in Czechoslovakia and the Serbs in Yugoslavia, who generally took charge. As before, countries were multinational: Yugoslavia had nine nationalities; Czechoslovakia seven. The map drawing by the Allies had left millions of people under alien rule: perhaps 9 million Magyars, Germans, and Ruthenes alone.

To deal with the problem that they had left unresolved, the Allies wove a web of "minorities treaties" under the

League of Nations. These were intended to provide legal protection for the minority populations of Central and Eastern Europe, and elsewhere. The governments against which claims could be lodged deeply resented these treaty obligations as an interference with sovereignty. By and large, in the twenty years that followed, the treaties did not work. Either the guaranteeing powers sat by, doing nothing, and allowed minorities to be abused or massacred because they had no political interest that would be served by interfering; or they had an interest, and went ahead to serve it, as Nazi Germany was to do by using the protection of the German minority as an excuse for destroying Czechoslovakia in 1938 and 1939. As will be seen, the Balkan settlement left the area prone to internal and external insecurity.

15

EXCHANGING POPULATIONS

A T THE FRINGES of the Balkans, a terrible drama took place that shed light on the inadequacies of the Balkan settlement.

In August 1920, representatives of the Ottoman sultan signed the Treaty of Sèvres, formally ending the war with the Allies and ratifying the loss of Turkey-in-Europe (except for a small perimeter around the city of Constantinople). In Asia Minor, however, the Allies encountered resistance to their program of dismembering the country. An Allied army of occupation in Constantinople suppressed dissent from the Ottoman Chamber of Deputies and what remained of the government. In Smyrna, the great Christian port city of the Mediterranean coast, a Greek army deputized by the Allies stood guard over the interests of a Greek population that had settled there nearly three thousand years before.

But in the interior, nationalist forces led by a war hero,

General Mustafa Kemal, rallied to the cause of a Turkish state separate from the sultan's cosmopolitan empire, and they rejected Allied plans for their future as embodied in the Treaty of Sèvres. The British were unable to take effective action, having already demobilized their army, and so in March 1921 British prime minister David Lloyd George encouraged the Greek government to launch an offensive from Smyrna into the Turkish interior to crush Kemal's rebellion.

The Greeks moved forward to the attack on July 10, 1921, and scored brilliant successes as they drove ahead through the summer. They were stopped only in front of the rebel capital city, Angora, today's Ankara. Both sides fought to the point of total exhaustion. The Greeks then withdrew.

A year later, Kemal's Turks drove through Greek defenses on the coast in a surprise attack that disorganized the defenders and sent them reeling. Turning north, the Turkish armies then rolled up the entire Greek-held coastline in a march toward Constantinople. Smyrna went up in flames, and an ethnic war that had been characterized by brutalities and atrocities all along now threatened an entire population with mass deportation or mass murder.

Greece and its sponsor, Great Britain, capitulated. A cease-fire in 1922 was followed by a full peace agreement at Lausanne in 1923, recognizing Kemal's state as the government of Turkey and ratifying the demise of the Ottoman Empire. Kemal would soon take the name Ataturk, or "Father Turk," as recognition of his status as father of his country.

Ever since the first two Balkan Wars, waves of refugees had been emigrating and immigrating as frontiers changed in the former Ottoman realms. No fewer than seventeen migratory movements had taken place in Macedonia alone in the years since 1912. The new boundaries being drawn at Lausanne stranded 1.3 million Greek refugees from what had been the Ottoman Empire. Turkey would not allow them to return.

On December 1, 1922, Dr. Fridtjof Nansen, a Norwegian winner of the Nobel Peace Prize, declared that a mass flight of refugees on that scale was irreversible. He proposed that the exodus be treated as a fait accompli, but that it should provide the basis for a population transfer that would be mutual. The suggestion was taken, and Greece expelled 400,000 Turks. Matters relating to the treatment of the refugees and their assets were regulated by treaty, as they had been in an earlier (1913) population exchange between Greece and Bulgaria and one following the terms of the 1919 Treaty of Neuilly, which had ended hostilities between the Allies and the Bulgarians, ceding Bulgaria's Aegean coast to Greece.

Nansen's proposal was called a population "exchange," but that was a cosmetic term. In fact, it was compulsory. Article I of the convention between Greece and Turkey stated that, subject to defined exceptions, "As from 1ˢᵗ May, 1923, there shall take place a compulsory exchange of

Turkish nationals of the Greek Orthodox religion established in Turkish territory, and of Greek nationals of the Muslim religion established in Greek territory. These persons shall not return."

Ernest Hemingway, a young newspaper correspondent for the *Toronto Star*, had witnessed a line of refugees twenty miles long streaming out of Asia Minor, and said that he could not get it out of his mind. Michael Llewellyn Smith, a recent historian of these events, has written that "No one wished to take credit for initiating the idea of a compulsory exchange, so repugnant to liberal principles. But the measure solved the age old problems of the minorities at a stroke." Looking back, the editors of *Foreign Affairs* commented in 1972 that "while such exchanges of minorities may indeed permanently resolve past discords, it would be a rash, or callous, statesman who would urge population transfers as a solution: the human costs were tremendous."

It was an operation that, though conducted without anesthetics, saved a life. In 1945 that was brought back to mind, as statesmen focused not on the memory of almost unimaginable pain but on the fact that the patient had been cured. After World War II, the Allied victors again redrew boundaries in Europe, but in addition expelled whole populations. Russia, Poland, Czechoslovakia, and Hungary forcibly deported literally millions of inhabitants. And this time the settlement held.

16

THE ATTACK ON YUGOSLAVIA

YUGOSLAVIA WAS ONE of the outstanding creations of the postwar peace settlement. It came out of World War I, and from the start was challenged by those disappointed in the outcome of that war.

Yugoslavia and its neighbors began their postwar lives by fearing the designs of Hungary. The Hungarians had been one of the two ruling peoples of the Austro-Hungarian Empire; they were major losers both in the war and in the peace settlement. It would be only natural for them to want to regain some of what they had lost. And so in 1920–21 Yugoslavia banded together with Czechoslovakia and Romania to form a mutual defense arrangement known as the "Little Entente." It looked for support to France. To a limited extent, and for a limited time, it was able to supply France with a potential ally to take the place of tsarist Russia should another German war arise. The alliance also served to hold Hungary's ambitions at bay, allowing the new borders to harden in the public mind.

★　★　★

Italy, which had emerged from the war a disappointed winner, coveted territorial gains across the Adriatic at the expense of Albania and Yugoslavia. It was a tangled situation, for Albania's rising leader, Ahmed Bey Zogu (who later would claim royal status as King Zog), had worked with Yugoslavia against the leaders of the Albanian Kosovo independence movement. Later vicissitudes led Zog to shift from Yugoslav to Italian support.

From 1922, Italy was in the hands of Benito Mussolini, the sometime Socialist who had founded the Fascist movement and led it to power. A political agitator who called himself "an adventurer for all roads," he exploited the enthusiasm of the Italian public for glory and empire.

At times, Mussolini acted as the patron of Albania against the Yugoslavs. At other times, it is widely believed, he sent arms and money to Macedonia and Croatia to subvert Yugoslavia from within and without.

Yugoslavia's eastern neighbor, Bulgaria, also posed a threat, for a powerful military clique within the country continued to reject the settlement of the Congress of Berlin (1878) and to regard Macedonia as the southern half of Bulgaria. The conspirators—known as the External Organization—organized raids into Macedonia with the aim of disrupting the Yugoslav state. Their competitor was the notorious Internal Macedonian Revolutionary Organization (IMO), which had been founded in 1893 in Salonika, alongside the Young Turks and other secret societies. Its aim was an independent Macedonia. The External and Internal organizations had split into a variety of factions whose terrorist attacks horrified Europe in the 1920s and 1930s.

These shadowy organizations intrigued also to bring about a militarist regime in Bulgaria. While it was not always clear whether it was Bulgaria injecting violence into Macedonian politics, or the other way round, it was evident that the conspirators opposed the governments both of Yugoslavia and of Bulgaria, and hoped to destroy the good relations between them.

Fascist Italy is believed to have encouraged and subsidized these activities. Several attempts were made by the terrorist groups to assassinate Bulgaria's pro-Allied and reformist prime minister, Alexander Stambulisky, the architect of Bulgarian-Yugoslav friendship. Finally, in 1923, army officers staged a successful coup d'état and executed him. He was replaced by a military-controlled regime dangerous to Yugoslavia.

★   ★   ★

Insecure externally, Yugoslavia also was shaky from within, as the hoped-for bonding between Serbia and Croatia did not take place. Hamilton Fish Armstrong, managing editor of *Foreign Affairs,* reported in the pages of his magazine in 1922 what had been said by the most charismatic of the Croat leaders: "that though the Serbs, Croats, and Slovenes probably have to live together, the bonds between them must be as shadowy as possible and each province must go its own way—politically, commercially, culturally." In his article, and in a book that he wrote several years later, Armstrong was oddly hopeful. It was not ancient feuds that pulled these peoples apart, he said, but politics. They would be able to work together if they saw that it suited their interests to do so. But his report did not entirely support that conclusion. The Serb and Croat politicians rarely worked together in practice, and the Serbs did not seem disposed to share power.

Tensions rose. Several Croat members of parliament were murdered. Despairing of politicians, King Alexander abolished the constitution and declared himself dictator in 1929.

Mussolini opened secret training camps in Italy where Croatian terrorists were taught to use weapons and explosives for use against Serbia. The largest group among the Croatians were the Ustashe, a Fascist ultra-nationalist society.

On October 19, 1934, while in Marseilles making a state visit to France, King Alexander was killed by Croatian gunmen. The assassins were carrying money and passports provided by the Italian government, and they were acting under the orders of the Ustashe leader, Ante Pavelic.

★   ★   ★

In the interwar years, the Yugoslav government tried to make the Kosovo problem go away. Kosovo was a newly gained territory, conquered in 1912, lost immediately afterwards, and retaken from the Ottomans at the end of the war. The problem was that the population was overwhelmingly Albanian Muslim.

The Yugoslav government initiated programs to settle Serbs on the land. It also refused to be bound by League of Nations commitments to safeguard minority rights. It closed the Albanian Muslim school system. It confiscated Kosovar lands. It made conditions discouraging enough so that many Kosovars left the country, though a sizable number remained. On the eve of World War II, Yugoslavia was about to negotiate a treaty with Ataturk's successors in Ankara, whereby Yugoslavia would forcibly deport Muslims and Turkey would take them in, at a fixed price per family. Then the war intervened.

★ ★ ★

Nazi Germany began its 1941 spring campaign season early. Its armies crossed the Danube on pontoon bridges on March 1. They passed through friendly countries, Hungary, Romania, and Bulgaria, en route to the Mediterranean.

Before dawn on April 6, 1941, German warplanes struck crippling blows at Yugoslavia and Greece. It was blitzkrieg warfare: the Yugoslav Army surrendered on April 17. King Peter, the country's monarch, flew off on a British Royal Air Force flying boat and established a government-in-exile in London.

Riding in with the Germans and sharing in their triumph was the Croatian Ustashe leader Ante Pavelic, who became Croatia's wartime dictator and participated in the killing of a half million Serbs.

Others in Yugoslavia resisted Fascist rule. Accounts still

differ as to the wartime effectiveness of the rival Yugoslav resistance groups, the Chetniks loyal to King Peter, or the Communist-led partisans of Josip Broz (who became better known by his nom de guerre, Tito). Much of their time and energy seems to have gone into their wars against one another. Even so, they stood their ground against the foreign invaders.

After the war, it was Tito who emerged the winner. Unlike his interwar predecessors, he somehow was able to suppress ethnic conflict by imposing his own brand of communism. For administrative purposes, he tossed the nationalists a bone by dividing the country into six republics, following the pre–World War I borders of Slovenia, Croatia, Bosnia-Herzegovina, Serbia, Montenegro, and Macedonia. But all true power resided with him in the federal capital, Belgrade—although scholars today suggest that the regime was more complex than that might suggest. And in 1974, when he suspected that the Serbs were getting too powerful, he carved out two autonomous regions from Serbia's territory: Vojvodina in the north, with a large ethnic Hungarian population; and Kosovo in the south, populated mostly by ethnic Albanians. The Serbs groused, but acquiesced.

At the time of Tito's death in 1980, it had become clear to most observers that Yugoslavia was a country, and a region, where national conflict had been superseded successfully only by empires. There had been Rome, there had been Byzantium, there had been Ottoman Turkey, and there had been Tito. What would come next was an open question.

PART VI

AMERICA'S JOURNEY TO

THE FRONTIERS

17

RETURNING TO THE SCENE
OF THE CRIME

UP UNTIL 1989, international politics largely followed from World War I. World War II flowed from World War I: and the Cold War from World War II. The century-long epidemic of communism developed from the virus planted by the German General Staff in Russia in 1917, in the political equivalent of bacteriological warfare. (The Germans had granted safe passage to the train carrying Lenin from Zurich to Petrograd, in hopes that he would seize power and take Russia out of the war.) The imbalance in power between Germany and its neighbors, which had tempted Berlin to start two world wars, also was at the heart of the Cold War; for neither West nor East could let the other side possess Germany. The transition from a horse-drawn world to a planet that sends rockets into space was driven by military expenditures on technology during the Great War and its successors.

In the decade beginning with 1989, it looked as though

history at last had broken free from the 1914–18 war and the Paris Peace Conference that followed it. Promises broken and hopes crushed by the warmakers and peacemakers of long ago now could be restored to the world's agenda, and once again the United States seemed to be on the verge of leading the world across a frontier into a changed and better era. President Bush's words, echoing Wilson's, resonated: there was to be a "new world order." The United Nations supposedly was demonstrating new resolve in Iraq in 1990–91, where aggression, we were told, was being repulsed and punished, and justice was being done.

Instead, what has been happening in the 1990s, at least in some parts of Central and Eastern Europe, is a return to the politics and passions of *before* 1914. It is as though all movement in that part of the continent had been frozen by the various Fascist and Communist regimes for decades; and now, with the ice melting away, has resumed. It could easily be imagined that the twentieth century was time off, an intermission from history; and that Woodrow Wilson, Theodore Roosevelt, Thomas Masaryk, Georges Clemenceau, David Lloyd George, and the very young Winston Churchill were just leaving their dressing rooms to strut back upon the stage.

As the world approached 2000, it was warned of a possible computer disaster. By now, everyone will have heard of the Y2K problem. The problem to which it referred was that unless reset, many computers on the eve of the century, instead of going ahead to 2000, could turn around, go back, and start again at 1900.

So it is with Yugoslavia, unless someone resets it. Instead of being linear, its history threatens to be circular, going round back to the beginning, and never straight ahead to cross the frontier into the future. And so it could be for the outside powers, if again they allow themselves to be drawn in, to play out their own game of power politics on Balkan soil.

Nationalism, the forbidden passion under Tito's Communist regime, as it had been under the Habsburgs and Ottomans, again threatens to shatter the political structure of southeastern Europe and to destroy its peace. Ethnic fanaticism threatened the old Europe; it now threatens the new. The shots fired in the Bosnian capital of Sarajevo in the 1990s came from the same gun as those fired in 1914. The Russian poet Yevgeny Yevtushenko has expressed in a telling phrase what is happening now in the Balkans. In *The New York Times* on May 1, 1999, he wrote that, like the murderer in *Crime and Punishment,* "history returns to the scene of its crime."

★ ★ ★

The events starting in 1989 in the Soviet Union moved in curious parallel with those in Yugoslavia. Both countries were Communist multinational states, and both had started to come unraveled in the 1980s. The United States took an interest in seeing that both evolved in a way that did not threaten international peace and stability. The American preference, in George Bush's day as in Woodrow Wilson's, was for countries to remain united and intact. America was afraid of out-of-control nationalism.

In a speech delivered in Kiev, the ancient Ukrainian capital, in August 1991, Bush warned that "freedom is not the same as independence. Americans will not support those who seek independence in order to replace a far-off tyranny with a local despotism. They will not aid those who promote a suicidal nationalism based upon hatred." He added that "We will support those who want to build democracy."

The breakup of the Soviet Union into many small, relatively powerless states would of course remove what had been a long-standing threat to the United States. At a cabinet meeting a month following the Kiev speech, Secretary of Defense Richard Cheney made that point: it would be best if the successor states to the Soviet Union were democratic; but "If democracy fails, we're better off if they're small." To which Secretary of State James Baker countered: "The *peaceful* breakup of the Soviet Union is in our interest. We don't want another Yugoslavia."

There was a certain confusion among the several American objectives that had been adopted in pursuit of a new world order. The breakup of the Soviet Union was a process that held high national security concerns for the United States; but in the post-Communist era, the fate of Yugoslavia did not.

Moreover, as the Yugoslav crisis was brought to its attention, the Bush administration in 1990 and 1991 was preoccupied with the Gulf War against Iraq. And as Warren Zimmermann, then the American ambassador to Yugoslavia, noted in his memoirs, "Even a great power has difficulty in dealing with more than one crisis at a time." So, while the Soviet situation received priority, the Yugoslav crisis did not—at a time when action should have been taken, according to some observers, if it were to be taken at all.

It was in regard to the Soviet Union in the decade starting in 1989 that the United States felt liberated, and free at last to go forward to change the world in the ways it deemed best. In counterpoint, events in Yugoslavia in those years served as a reminder of stubborn realities that refused to go away, even when faced with America's new and unprecedented accumulation of power.

★   ★   ★

When Warren Zimmermann was sent out from Washington to Belgrade in 1989, he could not have known that he would be the last accredited envoy to the country that had been proclaimed in 1918. He did know that he arrived at a time of change. He planned to state openly, on arrival, that Yugoslavia "no longer enjoyed the geopolitical importance that the United States had given it during the Cold War." That was true at the time, and Zimmermann could have had no idea that American armed forces would be sent into action in that country. On a more prescient note, Zimmermann did observe that "human rights had become a major element of U.S. policy, and Yugoslavia's record on that issue was not good—particularly in the province of

Kosovo, where an authoritarian Serbian regime was systematically depriving the Albanian majority of its basic civil liberties."

Zimmermann's instructions were to reassert the longstanding U.S. position in support of unity, independence, territorial integrity, and democracy. It transpired that these four goals were not necessarily compatible in Yugoslavia. Driven by demagogues, the voters were polarized along ethnic lines that within two years would lead to the breakup of their country, so that unity and territorial integrity were on one side, democracy and independence on the other. The paradox was that the stated purposes of the United States would have been better served by a dictator like Tito than they were by a democracy.

Somehow Tito, half-Croat and half-Slovene, had kept the country together. Accounts of how he did it differ; but after his death in 1980 the structure of the state survived in the form of a loose federation with a rotating presidency. Communism was not working; indeed, people throughout the world had lost faith in it. The party apparatus might be real, but the party ideology was not.

Into this situation a Serbian party Communist functionary named Slobodan Milosevic intruded himself. Milosevic went on an official trip to the village of Kosovo Polje in 1987. On April 24, he visited the local Ministry of Culture, where he was scheduled to deliver a speech, having brought along television crews from Belgrade. Outside the building, local Serb nationalists staged an event. With stones and steel rods, they attacked the local police, who were Albanian Kosovars, deliberately provoking the police to beat them back. Milosevic, who had been standing on a balcony, rushed down, waded into the crowd, and cried, "No one should dare to beat you!" "Slobo! Slobo!" chanted the crowd in response. The scene was broadcast and rebroadcast by Serbian television, establishing Milosevic's reputation as a man with a grasp of the uses of the media. A star was born—or so, at least, runs the story.

Milosevic campaigned for higher office in what sounds like an American fashion, organizing mass meetings and media events. By the end of the year he was the leader of Serbia. American observers tended to evaluate Milosevic as a cynic who was riding the crest of a nationalist wave. By way of contrast, they characterized the Croatian leader, Franjo Tudjman, as a genuine nationalist. As leaders of the two main peoples of Yugoslavia, both men played a major role in the complex maneuverings of the 1990s, during which Yugoslavia did indeed come undone.

Slovenia, Croatia, and Macedonia chose and achieved independence in the early 1990s. Even Montenegro showed signs of perhaps going its own way. Bosnia tried to do so, but was pinned down in a three-way civil war among its Muslim, Serb, and Croat populations, with crucial roles being played by Serbia and Croatia.

On March 3, 1992, Bosnia-Herzegovina proclaimed itself an independent country. Its leader, Alija Izetbegovic, was a Muslim, as were a plurality of its people. Bosnia's Christian Serb and Croat communities, sponsored more or less covertly by, respectively, Serbia and Croatia, took up arms against their new government. Controversy still surrounds the aims of these rebels: whether each aimed at autonomy or independence for itself, or whether they aimed at forming part of, respectively, Serbia and Croatia.

What is clear is that the Bosnian civil war was waged with an animal ferocity that shocked the Western world. The conflict gave the world a new and terrible phrase: "ethnic cleansing." It meant using mass murder, mass rape, and mass deportation to clear an area of minority populations. Reports differ, as they always do, but the Bosnian Serbs seemed to be the ones leading the way in practicing such atrocities.

The war raged on for three years.

★ ★ ★

According to the school of Rebecca West, history still lives in the Balkans. Ghosts haunt; feuds never die. No nation, no clan, will live in peace with one another. Nationalism is the force that drives history in these fierce Slavic lands.

The United States, however, is the country that does not believe in history. Americans are people who came from somewhere else and started fresh, with a clean slate, unencumbered by the past.

It may have been their native inclinations that led American observers of the Balkan scene to view West's thesis with a skeptical eye. It was the politicians, they reported, who destroyed Yugoslavia by deliberately arousing nationalism. Television programs in the various Yugoslav republics are said to have sown fear that neighboring groups would commit atrocities—and in turn incited the committing of atrocities against those neighboring groups as a preemptive act, to protect home and family.

Perhaps. The years of televised fearmongering certainly must have had their effect. Yet how could Milosevic, Tudjman, and others have successfully appealed to the nationalism of the voters if the nationalism wasn't there in the first place?

★   ★   ★

The tactics and strategies of the Bush and Clinton administrations, in conjunction with allies within and outside the Balkans, supported by all the power the United States could apply, were unable to keep Yugoslavia together. One after another, its republics seceded and proclaimed independence. These included the multi-ethnic former Yugoslav republic of Bosnia-Herzegovina, which now became independent.

The United States fell back on the defense of the integrity of Bosnia-Herzegovina itself, as rebel ethnic groups threatened to carry the process of disintegration further. On the face of it, the United States succeeded, but the 1995 accords, negotiated at Dayton, Ohio, under American auspices, in practice partitioned that state along ethnic lines; the unitary state is a technicality rather than a reality.

Falling further back, the United States took its stand in Kosovo.

18

KOSOVO OR KOSOVA?

Kosovo (in Albanian parlance, Kosova) is a province of 4,200 square miles in southern Serbia, slightly smaller than the state of Connecticut. Its frontiers have shifted over the centuries. Figures are disputed, but its population as of a few years back was perhaps 2 million, of whom about 90 percent were of Albanian ethnic origin.

Kosovo used to have valuable mineral deposits, especially nickel, lead, zinc, and magnesium; but these are said to have been exhausted to some extent, and their current value is difficult to assess. The soil is, or was, rich; but over-population and over-farming have turned the area into a poor one.

Held by Ottoman Turkey for more than five centuries, Kosovo was regained by Serbia in 1912. Most of its population in modern times has been Albanian and Muslim, and they have had a history of harsh treatment by the Yugoslav authorities both before and after Tito.

Under Tito, in 1974, Kosovo was granted autonomy in a new Yugoslav constitution. Kosovo enjoyed its autonomy for nearly fifteen years. The autonomy was revoked by Belgrade when Slobodan Milosevic came to power.

A pattern developed in Kosovo in the 1990s of deadly repression by the authorities, followed by increased militance—"terrorism," according to Belgrade—on the part of the Kosovo Liberation Army (KLA) and Kosovar civilians. If you believed Serbia, it was the other way round: the provocations came first, followed by measures to suppress them.

It is a matter of dispute what Milosevic's intentions were in cracking down on the Kosovar people. He may not have intended to start a war. He may have planned to change the population balance in the province by applying pressure over a long period of time that ultimately would compel Kosovars to leave the country. He did try to settle Serbs in the province in large numbers, but that effort failed, as it had failed when tried by Serb leaders in the past. The Serbs may make much of their romantic attachment to Kosovo, but in real-world terms, it is an economically depressed area and therefore a less desirable place to live than other regions of Serbia.

In the summer of 1998, Milosevic found himself confronted by an armed KLA insurgency. Whether he regarded it as a serious threat or as an excuse for taking action, he moved to crush it. The United States and other countries, acting initially through the United Nations, moved to forestall another bloody conflict in Yugoslavia. In the end, the United States and its allies sponsored a peace agreement (negotiated in February 1999 at Rambouillet, in France) that the KLA signed only reluctantly, and that Serbia refused to sign at all.

Milosevic sent his troops and tanks into Kosovo. Led by the United States, NATO attacked by air on March 24, 1999. Serbia immediately undertook further "ethnic cleansing" in the province, forcibly deporting most of the Kosovar population. Whether Belgrade was responding to the NATO attack, or whether it merely went ahead to implement an ethnic cleansing program that it had planned in any event, remains the subject of dispute.

Ten weeks of NATO air attacks followed. On June 3, Milosevic in effect surrendered, and details of the surrender were confirmed in the military agreement reached June 9. But American and allied leaders remained wary as they approached a complex transition period.

So much is common knowledge. It briefly summarizes what we all know, or believe that we know, after reading our newspapers and watching our television sets.

In the preceding pages, some perspectives have been suggested for understanding this particular American involvement abroad. A few of them might be recalled here.

• Despite its physical location in Europe, Serbia (including Kosovo) can be usefully thought of, for many purposes, as part of the Middle East. For five hundred years it was governed by the Ottoman Empire. It was ruled by the sultan at the same time as was the Arab world, from North Africa to the Iranian frontier. It shares a common political formation with the countries of the Middle East. Its communities are used to dwelling in quarters of their own and to living separate lives. Nor do they have much experience of participatory democracy or traditions of responsible leadership.

- Yugoslavia's past needn't determine its future, but neither is its past forgotten or forgiven. The massacres, the betrayals, and the feuds can't simply be dismissed. Ethnic hatred may have been aroused or inflamed within the past few years by government-controlled television, but the gunpowder had to have been already there: lighting a match, as the politicians did, would not have ignited an explosion all by itself.

- The ongoing crisis should not be conceived as being confined to Kosovo. As the (London) International Institute for Strategic Studies reminded us in its *Strategic Survey 1998/99,* "At every stage of the Yugoslav war, which has lasted for almost a decade, the West dealt with the immediate crisis, but refused to look at the region as a whole."

- The ferment in southeastern Europe is a rebellion against the terms and principles of the peace settlement of 1920, coming out of the Paris Peace Conference of 1919.

- The United States continues to defend the principles of that peace settlement, and there is a real

question whether America is wise to do so in all circumstances.

This is the time to think about the rightness, not merely of
the American involvement in Yugoslavia but of the
choices that loom ahead. Which road should the United
States take? Here in Kosovo we, like Rebecca West, should
pause to meditate on the uses of power and on the achiev-
ability of goodness.

19

MAKING WAR:
THE OLD RULES AND THE NEW

AMERICANS HAVE BEEN told repeatedly, ever since Yugoslavia has become a focus of international concern, that this land is, in many ways, at the frontier. It is where Europe meets the Middle East, and where tomorrow is blocked by yesterday. We have been told more than once that the borders of the Roman Empire run through the Balkans, marking the line where civilization left off and barbarism began; and that the frontiers of Byzantium cut through here too, where Greek confronted Latin, where classical civilization divided, and where Christianity bitterly split itself in two. It is a land of sentry boxes and lookout towers, where, through the ages, shouts of alarm have resounded—often too late.

A high-water mark is there to be seen: a line that stretches from beyond Slovenia, in Austria, all the way south to Lepanto in Greece, traced by Ottoman civilization as it flooded to high tide, bringing with it another culture, another language, and another religion with six dozen sects.

Space-age Americans, watching on television and imagining themselves deplaning at Balkan airports, find themselves suddenly ushered into the fourteenth century. "What are we doing here?" they ask. Why go back to 1389, to the Field of the Blackbirds in Kosovo and to the wars of medieval Christianity against Islam? It's history—something in which Americans take little interest—and it's somebody else's history at that.

During the Cold War, we would not have gotten ourselves involved in a dispute like the one in Kosovo. In the days when the Soviet Union contained us, power realities would have kept us from interfering. It is because we are now free to indulge in backing up our ideals and sympathies with cruise missiles that we are there.

The United States *chose* to involve itself in the politics of Yugoslavia. It chose freely, having had no prior obligation to do so. It interfered in the internal affairs of another country: a practice condemned in traditional international relations. In disregard of the Charter, it chose not to act through the United Nations, choosing NATO instead. Breaking with another rule of public international law, the United States has gone to war against Serbia without formally declaring war.

In so doing, the United States is not serving any particular interest of its own. It is acting out of altruism. This is a new kind of approach to the use of power in world politics. It was called for by a line of U.S. presidents, from

Wilson to Bush and Clinton, who consider this to be a new era in world politics, in which the rules have changed.

* * *

In the old international relations, as we have known them until now, the essential use of a country's power has always been to provide it with national security. Generally speaking, only those countries that have enough power to win and then maintain their independence remain countries. The others tend to be absorbed by some other state. Having sufficient power to sustain sovereignty therefore is the common denominator of the entities—the independent countries—that take part in international relations.

Developing and assembling adequate power, and then putting it to work for self-defense, is not the only thing that countries do; but it is the one thing that they *all* do, and that they *must* do before they can go on to do anything else.

This fact may seem obvious. But it in effect was denied, at least in part, by Woodrow Wilson, who believed that in the future countries no longer would have to protect themselves unaided. Security, in his League of Nations plan, would be collective, as other countries would join to help repel any aggressor; no longer would each country need to maintain the armed forces to do so by itself.

Thinking themselves on the verge of a new world, the United States and Great Britain did disarm after World War I, with disastrous results. The practical education that the democracies subsequently received, as they survived the most blood-soaked of centuries, has since disabused them of this error.

We therefore may take it for granted that a country's primary concern is to be able to successfully defend itself against attack. It owes that to itself and to its citizens. But self-defense is a broader concept than the mere prevention or punishment of direct attacks on one's territory or citizens. "Vital interests" describes the category of what a state will defend, and ought to defend where necessary, by going to war. Country A defends its life—and has a right to do so, almost everyone will agree—when it keeps Country B from strangling it by cutting off necessary supplies of, for example, water or oil. The tricky thing, calling for fine judgment, is to detect and stop a threat to vital interests before it has fully developed and while it still can be nipped in the bud.

Thus, long before the American public recognized it, President Franklin D. Roosevelt in 1940–41 saw the need for an American forward defense. To wait until the Atlantic coastline was invaded, FDR saw, was to take arms too late. The United States was an oceanic power, and it was essential that the oceans themselves be dominated by the United States and its friends, and also that the far side of the Atlantic not be controlled by an expansionist enemy. It was there, on the far side of the ocean, that the United States and its Allies should take their stand, shielding the western hemisphere from attack. In Roosevelt's view, America's security frontier was not on the New England coast but on the Rhine.

Though contrary to common sense, FDR's views were vindicated by World War II. Afterwards, most observers agreed that it would have been easier to stop Hitler if the attempt had been made earlier. Having accepted this view without quite understanding it, Americans went on frequently to misapply it. It was true that if the Western democracies had stopped Nazi Germany at the Rhineland in 1936, Hitler would never have put the United States and its Allies in mortal danger a few years later. It also was true, as farsighted Americans said at the time, that if British Spitfires had succeeded in clearing the skies over London of Nazi warplanes, then American pilots would not be called upon to defend the skies over New York or Chicago or Los Angeles. Their fight was our fight, only they were fighting it for us.

But it was not then and is not now the case that any fight anywhere affects the United States. It was FDR, and not John Donne, who was vindicated by history. "Any man's death diminishes me, because I am involved in Mankind," wrote the seventeenth-century poet, and while it is true that sometimes another person's death *is* like a bit of one's self dying, too, it isn't always like that. Most of the time it makes good sense to ask for whom the bell tolls.

During the Vietnam War, President Lyndon Johnson used to tell visitors to the White House that if Saigon fell, Americans would have to dig in to defend the beaches of

Hawaii. That turns out to have been untrue. Saigon was lost; a quarter century has elapsed; and the only hordes that have invaded the beaches of Hawaii have been tourists.

★   ★   ★

As a general rule, the United States should go to war only to defend its vital interests. That is the traditional view. It also is supported by good reasons. For one thing, it is unwise to dissipate the country's strength and wealth by engaging in unnecessary conflicts. Strength and wealth should be husbanded for life-or-death situations, when they are absolutely needed. Then, too, avoiding unessential wars is in accord with the country's political philosophy, in which the government is meant to play a minimal role: the state is there only to provide the matrix of security that allows citizens to live their own lives and achieve their own goals.

Walter Lippmann once wrote, inaccurately but suggestively, that a vital interest is one that you're prepared to die for. The American government *has* a right to ask its citizens to die in battle in order that the United States may live; hence the United States can go to war to defend vital interests. But it is doubtful whether it is entitled to send us into battle in any other cause. As a general rule the government should not call upon its citizens to risk their lives except to protect the United States.

Of course, in international relations, there should be no inflexible rules. If war is proposed in aid of the national interest, though an interest less than a vital interest; and if the national interest argument is strong, and the cost of the operation in human lives looks to be minimal, then an exception should be considered. It is tempting to go ahead if it looks easy. But it looks easy so often—and it so rarely ends up being easy.

In a democracy, the vital interest requirement imposes a discipline of its own on governments. We saw it in action in the case of the American intervention in Somalia in 1992–93. As soon as television viewers in the United States saw the bodies of American soldiers being dragged through the streets, they—the members of the public—forced the administration to withdraw. The public usually will not allow the lives of our soldiers to be spent on any cause other than protecting the United States.

So the vital interest rule isn't just some sort of theory; it reflects a political reality. Not merely should presidents not send us into war for an interest that is not vital; they usually cannot do so for very long, for the public will insist on withdrawal.

The vital interest rule imposes its discipline in yet another way. In Vietnam, the United States attempted to have its way in a land in which we had no vital interest, but in which the indigenous forces that we opposed did have a vital interest. The enemy may well have been as wicked as we believed them to be, but the reason that after long years of combat the Americans quit and the North Vietnamese didn't was that they cared more than we did. They would pay any price, no matter how high; we wouldn't.

So, entering into a conflict with local forces, without a vital interest at stake, is not a favorable position for the United States. In such situations, even though it is bigger and stronger and can employ a futuristic inventory of high-technology weaponry, the United States is not necessarily well positioned to win.

This suggests that intervention in Kosovo was risky from the start, for it admittedly was not undertaken to protect America's vital interests. But other considerations caused the United States to lead a European alliance into combat against Serbia, and there was a good case to be made that the risks were worth running.

20

IMPOSING A NEW WORLD ORDER

ONE OF THE considerations animating the American leaders who involved the United States in the affairs of the former Yugoslavia was a desire to serve not the national interest, but the common interest of all countries in bringing peace and stability to the world.

As so often happens, it was with the best of intentions and with no selfish motives that America intervened in the Balkans. In the first instance, in the early 1990s we entered the scene to use our influence to prevent the breakup of the Yugoslav federation. Our basic view, derived from Wilson, was that all existing countries should continue to exist, and should do so within their existing frontiers, unless they consent to change the status quo.

This is a policy that would actively promote peace and stability. There is nothing wrong with this view. It may well have been right for the United States to advocate it in Yugoslavia. It may well be right for the United States to use

its best influence to secure support for the status quo elsewhere as well.

The American government is quite right to believe
that nationalism is dangerous; that changing the political
structure of the globe by force of arms is, by definition,
destabilizing; and that if every one of the five or ten thousand groups—our best rough current guess—that call
themselves "nations" were to win their independence, we
would find ourselves living in a geopolitical nightmare.
The world would never know a moment's peace in the
next thousand years, and we would end up with a planet
wracked by wars of independence and permanently un-
governable.

But some change in basic political structure is inevitable
over the course of years; and in a world of independent
states, it rarely will come about without a fight. In standing
in the way of all change, Wilson was rather like King
Canute forbidding the tides to rise. Though the United
States is right to support maintaining the integrity of existing countries, at the same time it could be wrong in trying to stand in the way of independence for nations that
are prepared to fight for it. It took a bloodbath for the
United States to hold itself together in the Civil War; it
would be an impossible task for the United States to hold
all the other countries of the world together as well.

The United States may be placing itself in losing situations by pushing the principle of sovereign integrity on
those who violently reject it. Thus in Kosovo today, the
United States pursues a goal that is opposed by both parties

to the conflict. Persuasive reports from the field tell us that the Kosovars now insist on independence—and we Americans are opposed to that. Our program is to restore the situation there to what it was in 1986: to bring back the deported population of the province, give it local autonomy, and then protect it against direct Serbian rule for an unspecified length of time.

Assume that the American program for Serbia-Kosovo were realized, and that our troops and those of our allies stood guard over such a settlement. If the KLA were to wage a terror and guerrilla war in Kosovo for independence, and police and military forces from Serbia were to attempt to infiltrate and repress the rebellion, the United States and its allies would be in the ludicrous position of having their local armed forces fighting against both sides in a foreign civil war.

★   ★   ★

American leaders of an idealist bent saw in the 1990s a window of opportunity to apply Wilsonian principles to the world. That is what George Bush and his colleagues said they were doing in 1991 when they threw back the Iraqi invaders of Kuwait.

But it took much of the assembled power of America and its allies to do so. Kuwait was the only occupied country that the United States has liberated since the end of the Cold War. America did not—could not—liberate, for example, Tibet from China.

The problem with Bush's "new world order," in which all invasions would be repelled, was that the United States doesn't have anywhere near enough power to carry it off. One solitary act of law enforcement does not impose a rule of law. One lone war against an invader does not achieve a new world order.

What is true of guaranteeing the countries of the world against external threat is true of protecting them from internal challenge, as is the case in Yugoslavia. The United States may be able to impose its will in Kosovo, but it hasn't the resources to impose its will in all the other potential civil wars to come, all around the world. There were valid reasons for waging war over Kosovo, but we are not going to be able to protect all the world's thousands of minorities against abuse or deportation, or all the world's two hundred or so countries against nationalist secessions.

Kosovo will not prove the rule, but it could prove the exception. Perhaps we ought to continue trying to tame both Serb and Kosovar nationalism; but we will establish no new world order by doing so.

21

PRESERVING CREDIBILITY

A S THE NEW American ambassador in Yugoslavia stated when he arrived in Belgrade in 1989, Yugoslavia was not high on America's list of geopolitical priorities. The United States was in favor of Yugoslavia remaining as it was, but its preservation was not a significant national interest of America's, let alone a vital interest.

In 1999, however, some political observers were attracted to the view that, while Yugoslavia's integrity had not been a vital interest before, it had *become* one. The argument was that a great power derives much of its ability to persuade and pressure others from the belief among other countries that the great power will back up its words with deeds and its requests with armed force. These other countries will generally give way without putting the great power to the test. Such, it is said, is credibility.

To preserve credibility, a great power that starts an intervention must carry through to victory. If it becomes discouraged and stops halfway, other countries, in the future, may feel emboldened to resist its wishes.

There is much truth in the argument. A country that bluffs soon gives itself away. And a power that shows itself to be easily deterred no longer enjoys serious consideration.

As applied to America in Yugoslavia, the argument was that, having entered into a confrontation with Serbia, the United States could not afford to back down, even if it was wrong to intervene in the first place. It is not an unreasonable argument, but there are several reasons for believing that it is not quite as persuasive as its proponents believe.

★   ★   ★

The United States is so much more powerful and wealthy than other countries that it need not worry as much as they do about this issue. America's greatness is palpable; it compels belief. The United States therefore can do things that others cannot. It surely can change course from time to time without losing its capacity to intimidate. If it made a practice of backing down, that would be a different matter; but it does not.

The credibility argument for staying the course until the goal is reached rests on the assumption that the goal *can* be reached. In our first approach to Yugoslavia, it turned out that we failed: the federation did break up into five independent countries. Even in Kosovo, and even on the morrow of victory, the United States may not obtain the outcome that it desires, in the long run, given that the American government wants an outcome that neither party to the dispute desires.

Finally, and perhaps most important, in warfare and in politics as in life, if you find that you are doing the wrong thing, it is best to stop doing it. You may receive credit for perseverance and strength of character for persisting in error, but little credit for intelligence. If the United States, upon finding that it is driving in the wrong direction, is too stubborn to turn around, surely it loses rather than gains in credibility: who would wish to follow such a leader?

One example out of the many possible: when General Charles de Gaulle returned to power as France's leader in 1958, his country was fighting a hopeless colonial war in Algeria. De Gaulle was brought to power largely by people who wanted to continue the war, and he himself believed in his nation's imperial grandeur. But the war was ruinous, so he cut the country's losses and ordered withdrawal. By doing so, he helped to arrest France's slide from greatness. He and his country were applauded and admired for having shown character and intelligence.

★   ★   ★

But, it is said, at issue in the Kosovo conflict was not only America's credibility but that of NATO, the alliance that the United States led into the Serbian intervention.

NATO's initial loss of credibility, however, was implicit

in the mission. NATO was formed as a defensive alliance, not as an enforcer of Western norms. Article 5 of the treaty that gave it birth was the heart of it: all parties to it agreed that an attack on one was an attack on all. It was evident that they meant it. It was right that they should mean it. It was in their interest to mean it. Nobody could doubt that they meant it. So the Soviet Union believed it—because it was true and it made sense. Any country that dreamed of attacking the approaches to the North Atlantic was on notice that every country in the alliance would fight back—because they would be fighting for their lives.

Quite rightly, the United States recognized the dangers in acting alone in Serbia—as the world's leading power it is envied and resented, and needs the cover of some grouping in order to defuse opposition—and there were reasons for acting through NATO. In the United Nations, after all, action would likely be blocked by Russia and China.

There were also positive reasons for valuing the contribution that NATO could make. Not least of these were staging grounds and launching facilities in the Adriatic region. As it happened, an additional benefit was the assumption of a leadership role by British prime minister Tony Blair, whose moral fervor and willingness to go the whole way exceeded, if anything, that displayed by the Americans.

But NATO, as it turned out, enjoyed no credibility in acting outside the role for which it was intended. Everybody believed that NATO members such as Norway and Holland would fight to the last against Soviet invaders of their soil, but nobody believed that they cared as much about the soil of Kosovo—or, put another way, that they cared as much about it as the Serbs or the Kosovars did.

That is why the Serbs did not take it for granted that if NATO planes threatened to fire, they would indeed fire. The Serbs made them go ahead and prove it.

And yet it was not to keep our credibility that most Americans supported taking action in Serbia. It was to save a million or more people from horrors of suffering, or from death.

22

A HUMANITARIAN SOLUTION

I F THE BALKAN PEOPLES at the center of the Yugoslav
crisis are haunted by ghosts, then so are the peoples of
the West, who have watched in anguish and have won-
dered what to do. In part, Europe and the United States
have felt called upon to do something because they did
nothing to halt the Armenian massacres, the Holocaust,
the Greece-Turkey mass deportations, the Pakistan-India
partition horrors, the Rwanda genocide. So many low
points in the history of the twentieth century weigh heavily upon the conscience of the West.

The burden of decision in Kosovo has therefore been
heavy. It has had to bear the weight of the past—and of the
future as well, for those who see in the post–Cold War era
an opportunity for America to change the world. It is
tempting to believe that, had we been there when those
earlier crimes against humanity were committed, we surely
would have done something to prevent them. Now we
have had a chance to prove it.

"Never again!" to the safe and secure Western world means that in the future we will not allow atrocities to be perpetrated. To the Jews of Israel, taught by tragedy to be more realistic than we are, it means just the reverse: it means that, no, the outside world would not step in to prevent a future genocide, and therefore each people must learn to defend itself from such a fate. Even after victory in Kosovo, the best that can be done is to punish some of the guilty and restore some of the refugees; the dead cannot be revived.

There *are* steps, however, that the outside world realistically can take to help victims of mass violence; steps that were not taken in such times as those of the Holocaust; and that, to the extent that the United States can afford it, Americans might well consider taking in regard to future Kosovos.

★   ★   ★

The way was pointed out by Jean-Henri Dunant, the nineteenth-century Swiss humanitarian who founded the Red Cross. He focused solely on alleviating suffering and kept to a strict neutrality. The Red Cross refused to take sides in armed conflicts; it tended to the wounded, no matter who they were. Hence its effectiveness in doing what it did.

Dunant's approach was to avoid politics. He made no attempt to overturn the results of combat. He did not challenge the acts of governments, no matter how objectionable. He did not try to change states or governments. It was a limited realm that he claimed for the activities of the Red Cross, but for that reason the organization was effective.

If we had acted according to these principles in the Kosovo matter, the United States and its allies would have reacted to the deportation of more than a million Kosovars from their homeland by concentrating on resettling them elsewhere and providing them with the means to start new lives for themselves. To some extent this was done; what is being considered here is whether it should have been done on a mass basis and *instead of* intervening militarily.

Of course it would have had to be done on a much larger scale than is now being contemplated. It might have been necessary for America and the rest of the world to welcome the immigration of all the almost 2 million Kosovars. And in similar crises in the future we would have to consider doing the same thing.

It is entirely consistent with a realist concept of American foreign policy for the country to intervene abroad militarily only in defense of its vital interests, but to give free play to its idealism and generosity by sharing some of its wealth with the homeless and dispossessed, and offering (along with other countries) to take them in.

Such a policy would take the unrealistic idealism out of foreign policy politics (where it sometimes can endanger the country) and would confine the doing good to purely humanitarian pursuits.

Of course there would be domestic opposition, for a number of reasons, some of them not admirable. Many

Americans were upset even by the original U.S. offer to take in a mere twenty thousand Kosovar refugees. That opposition would define the extent to which the United States is prepared to be humanitarian rather than self-interested.

What is morally inconsistent is to be unwilling to resettle Kosovars in the United States, but—supposedly on humanitarian grounds—to support military intervention to restore them to their homes: a course of action that involved loss of life. Preferring that people die rather than have someone thought to be undesirable move into your neighborhood may be human nature, but it is not humanitarian.

★   ★   ★

A realist American policy would have been non-intervention in Kosovo, on the grounds that the United States has no interests in the former Yugoslavia that would justify involving itself in the region.

A purely humanitarian American foreign policy, which is not inconsistent with the realist one and could have served as a complement to it, would have been to ignore the causes of the mass deaths and uprootings and to focus on saving the living, nursing the victims, and giving them new homes and new lives.

But there is another viable option—and it is the one the Clinton administration chose. Is it working in Kosovo? Will it work in other Kosovos to come?

23

IN SEARCH OF JUSTICE

IN WAGING WAR in the Balkan skies, the Clinton administration sought to open up a new option for the United States. Not only would America defend its security and its interests worldwide, and give expression (to the extent that it chooses) to its humanitarian instincts by taking in the homeless and the dispossessed, but it would also occasionally satisfy its urge to bring justice to the otherwise lawless world of international politics.

Relying on airpower, NATO forces led by the United States punished Serbia for what Americans regarded as wrongdoing, and pressured it into accepting the peace terms imposed by the allies in June 1999. Punishment and pressure: these, the Clinton administration has shown, are what NATO bombardments can bring.

Prevention still lies beyond our powers. Mass murders, mass rapes, and mass deportations can be accomplished long before the United States can organize an air armada to oppose them. Nor can America punish or pressure wrong-doers who are powerful or who are backed by powerful allies.

Then, too, the American-led air forces needed some help from ground forces capable of drawing out the defenders from their shelters. The KLA performed that service in Kosovo.

Costs set limits of their own. In the literal budgetary sense, the United States and its allies presumably can afford whatever they are out of pocket for the air war. What they will have to pay, in every sense, for occupation costs that could continue well into the twenty-first century is another matter; and so is the question of how many Kosovos NATO can afford to deal with at one time.

There are political costs to be reckoned, too, but these will not be visible for a long time. The governments of Germany and Russia, each in its own way, were helpful to the Clinton administration in pressuring the Yugoslav government to negotiate peace, but their peoples were estranged; whether there will be consequences, and if so, what they will be, are things we cannot yet know.

The Kosovo campaign shocked Western Europeans into a realization of their dependence upon American military resources. On June 3, the same day that the Serbian parliament voted to accept the peace proposal, the leaders of fifteen European countries announced that they had decided to build a self-sufficient military power of their own, as a result of the Balkan experience. Whether they in fact will go ahead to carry out their decision remains to be seen. If they were to do so, it is not clear whether on balance that would be a good thing or a bad thing for the United States.

★   ★   ★

Rebecca West's almost impossible dream of power disposed to do good has come true. The world's strongest country had put its might at the service of decency and right. With many qualifications, the United States can provide humanitarian relief to the victims of world politics and sometimes can punish international wrongdoers and pressure them to stop doing wrong.

But even within the indicated limits, West's dream-come-true brings less happiness then might have been supposed. For both "power" and "good" turn out to be ambiguous terms. Television watchers and newspaper readers in the United States had no difficulty in recognizing wickedness at work when they saw images of the Kosovar population being uprooted and deported by Serbs venting their hate, fear, and rage on longtime enemies. But oddly enough, people elsewhere viewed matters differently. In other countries television viewers and newspaper readers watched American bombs and missiles raining down on Serbian cities and civilians, and concluded that *Americans* were the war criminals.

The allied military administration of Kosovo and its successor UN interim civilian administration of the province will have to face this question of what is "good" in the context of Balkan politics as a whole. We can agree that what the Milosevic regime has done—its ethnic cleansing in Kosovo—was evil and should be undone. But it is by no means clear whether helping the cause of Albania or of the KLA or of any other enemy of Milosevic would be a good thing.

Irony is the theme of history. Policies frequently do not achieve what they were intended to achieve; not uncommonly, they achieve the reverse. So there is reason to fear that what will come out of our intervention will be something we did not intend.

Even if the results of our intervention in the Balkans were to be those for which we would wish, would we be doing good—at the price? For bombing Serbian cities and killing Serbian civilians are evils the United States has visited upon helpless people in order to achieve the higher good. Are we sure the good is higher?

★ ★ ★

Then there is the question of power. Americans in the past depreciated the role of power in world politics. For that reason or for another, we failed to match goals with the power needed to achieve them.

Now, however, we seem to have learned that lesson. The 1999 aerial bombardment of Serbia, however wise or unwise it may have been, was an action that it was within the power of the United States to undertake. But whether the remaking of Serbia is within our power is another question: and that is the question that arises now.

The weapons that make the United States so much more powerful than the other countries are exemplified by the air-to-air missiles referred to in the prologue. ("That's what your tax money goes for, sir.") They are useful in combat against the forces of a foreign country, but they are useless in governing a foreign people. Our power can accomplish some things but not others.

You cannot administer a society day to day by force alone. That is what the Anglican prelate William Ralph Inge (1860–1954) meant when he wrote that "A man may build himself a throne of bayonets, but he cannot sit on it."

American and NATO military force compels Serbia to agree that Kosovo will be administered for years to come by an international authority, one likely to bear the stamp of the United States. As trustee and guardian for Serbia's southern province, the authority will have to look at its role in context—political problems don't necessarily stop at the border, and commitments have a way of expanding. We may think the intervention is restricted to Serbia, but it could well spill over into many or all of the states of the Balkans. Overall, there is the problem that brought the United States, and later NATO, to that part of the world: restless Serbian nationalism and expansionism. Following America's doctrine, the United States will be protecting Serbian sovereignty in Kosovo—while the KLA strikes out at Serbs and Serbs try to retaliate. Meanwhile Serbs will be intriguing to annex their part of Bosnia when the moment comes, against American desires and despite promises on paper.

The Kosovar population is ethnically Albanian. The Albanian question, raised at the Congress of Berlin more than a century ago, still hangs over the Balkans; and as guardians of 2 million Kosovars, the United States and its allies will be responsible for dealing with it. Miranda Vickers, a leading British expert on Albania, wrote recently that a majority of Albanians in Europe want to be unified within a single Balkan state, a Greater Albania. Such a program, if realized, would bring new boundaries to Serbia, Macedonia, Montenegro, and perhaps Greece. Opposing boundary changes, the international authority could be brought into collision with the population it will be governing. The international authority may also be drawn into protecting the Serbian minority within the new Kosovo from the Kosovar majority.

More: an underlying unsettling dynamic in the Balkans is the continuing Albanian population explosion, which propels Albanians into neighboring states at a rate that threatens to destabilize the political balance of those states. How will the United States address this problem?

Another point, though easily misunderstood, needs to be made. In the Greece-Turkey-Bulgaria population deportations of 1913–23, and in the population deportations in Eastern and Central Europe ordained by the Allies after World War II, millions of people were uprooted, dispossessed, and sent penniless and homeless on what, for many, were death marches. These were tragedies on a massive scale: in terms of numbers, greater than Kosovo many times over. Yet the point is, it worked. It settled the issue. Countries that couldn't tolerate minorities got rid of their minorities; and minorities that had been tormented and excluded were resettled amongst people who considered them to be their own.

If the United States and NATO had not intervened, the Serbs would have settled the Kosovo issue, by ethnic cleansing. The Kosovars would have been pushed into Albania and forcibly reunited with their own people. Kosovo would be owned and inhabited exclusively by Serbs. Monstrous though it would have been to let the Milosevic regime profit from its crimes, it would all be over.

What will happen when the international authority tries to impose the plan that America supports—a multinational state with legal protections for minorities? Plans like this have been tried often in Central and Eastern Europe and mostly have not worked, which is why the Allies discarded such plans after World War II in Czechoslovakia, Poland, and elsewhere. If this failed model fails again in Kosovo, then the United States and its allies will have obtained possibly the only outcome *worse* than letting Milosevic succeed in his monstrous scheme. The Kosovars will have undergone all the terrible suffering that Milosevic imposed upon them—and the issue won't even be settled. New rounds of butchery will await them.

★   ★   ★

The trusteeship-for-Kosovo concept comes at the wrong time in history. Regardless of our professed "disinterestedness" and "pure intentions," we will be imposing an international regime on a foreign population that will perceive that regime as imperialist—and it is too late for imperialism. Recent historical experience has shown that imperialists tend to become unpopular, no matter how well they administer their tasks. People prefer bad homegrown government to foreign government. If Americans believe that they and their allies will be welcome forever in Kosovo because they arrived as liberators and protectors, they might contemplate the example of Great Britain in Palestine between the two world wars. Britain's title and role was that of mandatory, or trustee, as the international authority's title and role will be under the American-imposed peace plan. Britain's assigned task was to foster a Jewish National Home in Palestine, but many members of the British administration nonetheless supported Arab opposition to that program. The result was that both Jews and Arabs organized armed revolts against Great Britain.

Will not much the same thing happen under a Balkan trusteeship? After all, the United States opposes the political goals of both sides. And the mountains of Yugoslavia make ideal guerrilla warfare country, for insurgents against the rule of any international authority.

In a war of attrition by local enemies, a UN- or NATO-led peacekeeping force will be at a disadvantage. Its reinforcements and supplies will have to come from far away. Moreover, there is the matter of economic attrition:

even very recently, the United States, for example, was using million-dollar cruise missiles to destroy ten-thousand-dollar Serbian tanks.

There also is a familiar point to be considered: the Albanians and the Serbs will be willing to fight on forever, because each considers Kosovo their country; but Americans and other members of the alliance will quit at some point because, when we come right down to it, we don't care very much who rules the province or what its boundaries should be.

Then there is the broader damage that the United States, as leader of the alliance and sponsor of the international authority, might suffer by injecting itself into Balkan affairs. The United States might be resented throughout the Slavic and Balkan worlds. All the countries that have been involved there over the years, from Germany to Russia, could well be alienated by the intrusion of an American influence within their traditional spheres of influence.

★   ★   ★

Serbia's apparent surrender in June 1999 was a triumph for the United States. But it was the easy part. If we stick to our goals, what comes next is likely to be much more difficult. It may be a long time, if ever, before we are justified in breaking open the champagne.

24

FRONTIERS THAT CANNOT BE CROSSED

To THE UNITED STATES in an earlier era, "frontiers" meant the opposite of what they signified to the rest of the world: they meant something open, not closed. Americans weren't stopped by their frontiers; they were beckoned onward. The western frontier was like tomorrow: no matter when you arrived at it, it already had moved on further. Indeed, it already was a twenty-four-hour ride down the road.

The country expected something similar when the Soviet Union, its great adversary in the post-1945 world, stopped blocking it and fell by the way. The road ahead looked clear, and America's leaders summoned us to cross over into a new era.

But a frontier is a kind of limit; and there are limits in political life, as in any other sort of life, that stop us from going further.

★   ★   ★

In commencing hostilities in Serbia, the United States chose not to ask the Security Council of the United Nations for its approval. There was a reason for this: Russia and China could have been expected to veto the American initiative. So the United States turned instead to NATO to provide the cover of collective action: a cover that is useful in soliciting public support.

But it was only procedurally that the veto was avoided. Russia and China still disapproved of what the United States was about to do, and as Russia and China remain among the world's great powers, attention must always be paid to their views. Indeed, it was only after Russia had been induced to participate that a peace process was initiated in the spring of 1999. For that matter, NATO approval and participation was more procedural and less substantive than might have originally been thought: Germany found itself politically torn, as did Italy, Greece, and other members of the alliance. This constrained America's freedom of action.

The United States is more powerful than any other single country, but it is probably not more powerful than the other great powers in combination. It can avoid procedural limitations—votes and vetoes and the like—but cannot escape the underlying facts of international life sometimes represented by votes and vetoes.

The United States is circumscribed by the world's power realities. It is constrained by the existing and the emerging balance of forces in the world. America can be stopped by a balance pitted against it, whether it chooses to recognize that limitation on its freedom of action or not.

★   ★   ★

Sometimes it is a cumulative effect that makes a country bump up against its limits. In America's case, the accumulation may come from an inability to walk away from our victories. In 1950, the United States repelled North Korea's attack on South Korea, but we still, a half a century later, keep an army on its frontier standing guard against a recurrence. The Cold War came to an end in the years 1989–94, but 100,000 American troops remain in Europe, protecting against we know not what. The United States won the Gulf War in 1991, but keeps an army in Saudi Arabia to prevent another invasion, and, besides, bombards Iraq fairly often because we never really settled that war.

Now American troops are to be assigned to duty in Kosovo. Nobody knows how long they will have to stay, or whether more will have to be sent someday.

It is a political truism that "the United States cannot be the world's policeman." As a matter of fact, whether or not it should be, the United States already *is* the world's policeman.

★   ★   ★

The apparent success of the 1999 air war in the Balkans may well encourage future presidents to dispatch airplanes and missiles to other corners of the earth in support of American values. It is a temptation that in most cases should be resisted.

Aircraft and weaponry are not usually an appropriate vehicle for our values. If anything, our visible military superiority alienates other peoples, and leads them to doubt the values in which Americans always have professed to believe—including democracy, disarmament, and peace.

Moreover, the power equations of the 1990s were uniquely favorable to President Clinton's initiative. There were no global forces of consequence to stand in his way. It is hard to believe that America's luck in being the world's sole superpower will last for long. The Kosovo war may turn out to be, for all we know, the last crusade of the sole-superpower age.

In addition to the external limits, we have to recognize the internal ones. If American troops remain in the Balkans for a long time, we may well be reminded of our limitations in dealing with complex foreign cultures. We may remember that we are also constrained by priorities within our own hemisphere or within our own country. There are limits to our strength and wealth, and more important, there are limits to our knowledge and wisdom. There are frontiers that cannot be crossed: not even by the United States, even at the height of its glory.

NOTES

1. A View from Kosovo

14 "*Black Lamb and Grey Falcon* drew me": Kaplan, 1993, 8.
15 "face of a young panther": Rollyson, 1996, 30.
15 "Rebecca had a rough tongue": Ibid., 13.
15 "Writers on the subject of August Strindberg": Ibid., 36.
16 "Oh, men are miserably poor stuff!": Ibid., 43.
16 "little disaster of a girl": Ibid., 37.
17 "a huge and dirty lie": West, 1941, 876–77.
19 "honour and freedom and harmony": Ibid., 912.
21 "I began to weep": Ibid., 913.
21 "prove themselves inferior to their opponents": Ibid.
22 "Not one of them, even the greatest": Ibid.

2. Powerless America

29 "Believing that in the long run": Fromkin, 1995, 19.

3. America Survives Both Enemies and Allies

42 "Roosevelt liked the idea": Gilbert, 1986, 496.
42 "all the skill and resources required": Young, 1998, 35.
42 "We persist in regarding ourselves": Ibid., 24.
47 "The events of 1989–91": Gaddis, 1997, 283.

Notes

6. The Containment of the United States

60 "moves where opposition is weak": Fromkin, 1995, 465.
61 "a fluid stream," "every nook and cranny": Hoge and Zakaria, eds., 1997, 163.
61 "a long-term, patient but firm": Ibid., 163.
61 "counter-force": Ibid., 164.
62 "recruiting, subsidizing, and supporting": Lippmann, 1947, 21.
62 "white-washed," "seen through rose-colored spectacles": Ibid., 22.
63 Wilson in 1919 foretold: Moynihan, 1990, 106.
66 "U.S. force should be used": Fromkin, 1995, 509.

7. America Unbound

72 "that this would be the first": Bush and Scowcroft, 1998, 303.
72 "our improving relations": Ibid.
73 "ran counter to": Ibid., 304.
73 "You are a force for moderation": Cockburn and Cockburn, 1999, 83.
77 "Unlike the other charnel houses": Newsweek, December 7, 1992.
79 "a hero's welcome": Newsweek, March 21, 1994.

9. The Middle East Shapes the Balkans

94 "was extremely fragile": Braudel, 1973, II, 663.
94 "Eventually Turkey created": Ibid., 665.

10. The Two Hundred Years' Crisis

99 "Turkey seems to be": Palmer, 1976, 167.

12. Redrawing the Map and Starting Over

119 "The home front likewise had collapsed": Herwig, 1997, 433.

13. Wilson's Principles in Action

122 "The governments now associated": Almond and Lutz, 1935, 25.
127 "The phrase is simply loaded": Cited in Schaeffer, 1990, 51.

page

130   "he did not believe in it": Lippmann, 1944, 173.

130   "To invoke the general principle": Ibid.

130   "brought to Paris many and diverse delegations": *Encyclopaedia Britannica,* 14th ed., s.v. "Conference of Paris."

131   "When I gave utterance to those words": Temperley, 1921, IV, 429.

131   "to inquire into ancient wrongs": Ibid., 433.

15. Exchanging Populations

140   "No one wished to take credit": Smith, 1973, 335.

140   "while such exchanges of minorities": Dexter, ed., 1972, 631.

16. The Attack on Yugoslavia

142   "an adventurer for all roads": Smith, 1983, 33.

143   "that though the Serbs, Croats, and Slovenes": *Foreign Affairs,* June 15, 1923, 89.

17. Returning to the Scene of the Crime

152   "freedom is not the same": Bush and Scowcroft, 1998, 515.

152   Cheney-Baker exchange: Ibid., 519.

153   "Even a great power": Cited in Holbrooke, 1998, 26.

153   "no longer enjoyed the geopolitical importance": Hoge and Zakaria, eds., 1997, 571.

153   "human rights had become": Ibid., 571–72.

155   "No one should dare to beat you!": *National Journal,* April 3, 1999, 873.

23. In Search of Justice

189   Miranda Vickers, a leading British expert: Vickers, 1998, xi.

BIBLIOGRAPHY

Albrecht-Carrié, René. 1938. *Italy at the Paris Peace Conference.* New York: Columbia University Press.

Almond, Nina, and Ralph Haswell Lutz. 1935. *The Treaty of St. Germain.* Stanford: Stanford University Press.

Armstrong, Hamilton Fish. 1926. *The New Balkans.* New York: Harper & Brothers.

Braudel, Fernand. 1973. *The Mediterranean World in the Age of Philip II.* 2 vols. London: Collins.

Bush, George, and Brent Scowcroft. 1998. *A World Transformed.* New York: Knopf.

Cockburn, Andrew, and Patrick Cockburn. 1999. *Out of the Ashes: The Resurrection of Saddam Hussein.* New York: HarperCollins.

Deak, Francis. 1942. *Hungary at the Peace Conference.* New York: Columbia University Press.

Dexter, Byron, ed. 1972. *The Foreign Affairs 50-Year Bibliography: New Evaluations of Significant Books on International Relations, 1920–1970.* New York: Bowker.

Elsie, Robert. 1997. *Kosovo: In the Heart of the Powder Keg.* New York: Columbia University Press.

Fromkin, David. 1995. *In the Time of the Americans.* New York: Knopf.

———. 1981. *The Independence of Nations.* New York: Praeger.

———. 1989. *A Peace to End All Peace.* New York: Holt.

Gaddis, John Lewis. 1997. *We Now Know: Rethinking Cold War History.* Oxford: Clarendon Press.

Gilbert, Martin. 1986. *Winston S. Churchill: Road to Victory, 1941–1945.* Boston: Houghton Mifflin.

Glendinning, Victoria. 1987. *Rebecca West: A Life.* New York: Knopf.

Herwig, Holger H. 1997. *The First World War: Germany and Austria-Hungary 1914–1918.* London: Arnold.

Hoge, James F., Jr., and Fareed Zakaria, eds. 1997. *The American Encounter: The United States and the Making of the Modern World.* New York: Basic Books.

Holbrooke, Richard. 1998. *To End a War.* New York: Random House.

Ignatieff, Michael. 1994. *Blood and Belonging: Journeys into the New Nationalisms.* New York: Farrar, Straus & Giroux.

———. 1998 *The Warrior's Honor: Ethnic War and the Modern Conscience.* New York: Holt.

Jelavich, Barbara. 1983. *History of the Balkans.* 2 vols. Cambridge: Cambridge University Press.

Kaplan, Robert D. 1993. *Balkan Ghosts: A Journey Through History.* New York: St. Martin's Press.

Kennan, George F. 1951. *American Diplomacy 1900–1950.* Chicago: University of Chicago Press.

Lewis, Bernard. 1995. *The Middle East: A Brief History of the Last 2000 Years.* New York: Scribner.

Lippmann, Walter. 1947. *The Cold War: A Study in U.S. Foreign Policy.* New York: Harper & Brothers.

———. 1943. *U.S. Foreign Policy: Shield of the Republic.* Boston: Little, Brown.

———. 1944. *U.S. War Aims.* Boston: Little, Brown.

———. 1998. *Kosovo: A Short History.* New York: New York University Press.

Malcolm, Noel. 1944. *Bosnia: A Short History.* New York: New York University Press.

Moynihan, Daniel Patrick. 1990. *On the Law of Nations.* Cambridge: Harvard University Press.

Palmer, Alan, and Veronica Palmer. 1976. *Quotations in History: A Dictionary of Historical Quotations c. 800 A.D. to the Present.* Hassocks, Sussex: Harvester.

Rollyson, Carl. 1996. *Rebecca West: A Life.* New York: Scribner.

Schaeffer, Robert. 1990. *Warpaths: The Politics of Partition.* New York: Hill & Wang.

Bibliography

Smith, Denis Mack. 1983. *Mussolini*. New York: Vintage.

Smith, Michael Llewellyn. 1973. *Ionian Vision: Greece in Asia Minor 1919–1922*. New York: St. Martin's Press.

Stavarianos, Leften Stavros. 1958. *The Balkans Since 1453*. New York: Rinehart.

Temperley, H. W. V. 1921. *History of the Peace Conference of Paris*. 6 vols. London: Froude/Hodder & Stoughton.

Vickers, Miranda. 1998. *Between Serb and Albanian: A History of Kosovo*. London: Hurst.

West, Rebecca. 1941. *Black Lamb and Grey Falcon: A Journey Through Yugoslavia*. New York: Viking.

Wolff, Robert Lee. 1956. *The Balkans in Our Time*. Cambridge: Harvard University Press.

Young, Hugo. 1998. *This Blessed Plot: Britain and Europe from Churchill to Blair*. Woodstock, N.Y.: Overlook Press.

INDEX

Index